EPHESIANS
Forty Days of Living in God's Power

TOM FRENCH

EPHESIANS: FORTY DAYS OF LIVING IN GOD'S POWER

Copyright © 2023 Tom French
All rights reserved

ISBN - 978-0-6453079-1-7
Ebook ISBN - 978-0-6453079-2-4

First published 2023 by Frendrussi Press
Melbourne, VIC, Australia

No parts of this publication may be reproduced, stored in a retrieval system, or transmitted in any form or by any means, electronic, mechanical, photocopying, recording, or otherwise, without the prior written permission of the copyright owner.

This book is sold subject to the condition that it shall not, by way of trade or otherwise, be lent, resold, hired out, or otherwise circulated without the publisher's prior consent in any form of binding or cover other than that in which it is published and without a similar condition including this condition being imposed on the subsequent purchaser. Under no circumstances may any part of this book be photocopied for resale.

All scripture quotations, unless otherwise indicated, are taken from the Holy Bible, New International Version®, NIV®. Copyright ©1973, 1978, 1984, 2011 by Biblica, Inc.™ Used by permission of Zondervan. All rights reserved worldwide. www.zondervan.com. The 'NIV' and 'New International Version' are trademarks registered in the United States Patent and Trademark Office by Biblica, Inc.™

The website addresses recommended throughout this book are offered as a resource to you. These websites are not intended in any way to be or imply an endorsement on the part of the author, nor does he vouch for their content.

This book was primarily created on the lands of the Wurundjeri people of the Kulin nation. The author pays respects to their Elders past, present, and future.

Cover illustration by Matt Baker

For Layla,
May you stand

Contents

Acknowledgements	9
Introduction to Pop's Devotions	11
Introduction to Ephesians	17

Day One: Everyone Loves Getting Letters   27
Ephesians 1:1–2

Day Two: Secret Billionaires   31
Ephesians 1:3

Day Three: Chosen Before Time   35
Ephesians 1:4–6

Day Four: 'Here's the Plan…'   39
Ephesians 1:7–10

Day Five: No Second-class Citizens   43
Ephesians 1:11–14

Day Six: The Menu   47
Ephesians 1:15–19a

Day Seven: Friends in High Places   51
Ephesians 1:19b–21

Day Eight: The Fullness   55
Ephesians 1:22–23

Day Nine: Diagnosis: Death   59
Ephesians 2:1–3

Day Ten: The Cliffhanger   65
Ephesians 2:4–7

Day Eleven: Famous   69
Ephesians 2:8–9

Day Twelve: Finding What You Were Made For   73
Ephesians 2:10

Day Thirteen: Left Out *Ephesians 2:11–13*	77
Day Fourteen: The New Human *Ephesians 2:14–18*	81
Day Fifteen: Feels Like Home *Ephesians 2:19–22*	87
Day Sixteen: Mystery Solved *Ephesians 3:1–6*	91
Day Seventeen: The Universe is Watching *Ephesians 3:7–13*	95
Day Eighteen: There's Always More *Ephesians 3:14–19*	99
Day Nineteen: The End of Part One *Ephesians 3:20–21*	103
Day Twenty: Unified With Them? *Ephesians 4:1–6*	107
Day Twenty-one: Socks and a Magic Axe *Ephesians 4:7–13*	111
Day Twenty-two: Are You Grown Up? *Ephesians 4:14–16*	117
Day Twenty-three: Living the Dream *Ephesians 4:17–24*	121
Day Twenty-four: People of the Truth *Ephesians 4:25*	125
Day Twenty-five: Getting Mad *Ephesians 4:26–27*	129
Day Twenty-six: Takers and Givers *Ephesians 4:28*	133

Day Twenty-seven: F-bombs and Other Weapons of Mass Destruction 137
Ephesians 4:29

Day Twenty-eight: The Sad Spirit 141
Ephesians 4:30

Day Twenty-nine: The Example 145
Ephesians 4:31–5:2

Day Thirty: The One About Sex 149
Ephesians 5:3a

Day Thirty-one: Showing Up 155
Ephesians 5:3–7

Day Thirty-two: Living Light 161
Ephesians 5:8–14

Day Thirty-three: Live for the Moment 165
Ephesians 5:15–21

Day Thirty-four: Relationship Revolution 171
Ephesians 5:21–33

Day Thirty-five: Parents Can Be Exasperating 177
Ephesians 6:1–4

Day Thirty-six: Slavery 183
Ephesians 6:5–9

Day Thirty-seven: Stand Your Ground 189
Ephesians 6:10–13

Day Thirty-eight: Armour Up! 193
Ephesians 6:14–17

Day Thirty-nine: Supply Lines 197
Ephesians 6:18–20

Day Forty: The End Credits 203
Ephesians 6:21–24

Bibliography 207
Get more Pop's Devotions 209
Also by Tom French 210
About the Author 213

Acknowledgements

When I started writing these devotions my wife was pregnant. Somewhere along the way our baby daughter popped out. Unsurprisingly, after that my progress on these devotions slowed right down. I had promised to have this book out by early 2021, but as I write this acknowledgement it's mid-2022, baby Layla has become toddler Layla, and the book isn't even published yet. Still, I'm very happy to have been delayed by being a dad. I hope all three of my fans have survived the wait. Thanks for turning up and giving me plenty of joy, Layla Joy!

One of the fun things I got to do while putting together these devotions was to share them with my youth group in their early draft form. They read them every week at youth group, and sometimes even during the week in between youth groups. They made suggestions for ways to improve the devotions, and some who have an eye for detail even pointed out my many grammatical errors. So a big thank you to the Inner North Youth Group for their help, and especially to James Thomas, Sasha Hodson, Sarah Hameed, Hannah B, Chris Beeck, Luke Bertram,

Callum Martin, and Aoife Martin, who showed me the errors of my typing ways.

John French, the Pop of Pop's Devotions, used a draft of this book to do his daily devotions. Pop's devotions were Pop's Devotions! How meta! Thanks for taking the time to read them and give me your wisdom, Pop!

Matt Baker did an excellent job on the cover art. I'm so pleased you gave your skills to creating the artwork. That angel and demon battle is awesome!

Once again, Jo Stockdale has done a great job editing these. Thanks for slogging away through the global pandemic to make sure this book is as good as it can be.

Thanks to Samantha Dunn, for proofreading the mistakes out of this and doing with great speed. Sometimes social media has not been a force for good, but I'm pretty glad I found a quality proofreader there.

My wife, Emily, is excellent and I love her. Thank you for all the love and support in helping me write, even when it's not the most convenient thing to be doing with my time. You're the best!

Finally, praise be to the God and Father of our Lord Jesus Christ, who has blessed us in the heavenly realms with every spiritual blessing in Christ. May you be glorified.

Introduction to Pop's Devotions

I love reading my Bible in the morning. It makes me feel great! I feel like a super-Christian for doing the thing that people have been telling me I should do all my life – reading my Bible. Unfortunately, however much like a super-Christian I may feel, I can often read huge chunks of the Bible and feel like I've not taken anything in. I may have understood all the words along the way, but I couldn't tell you much about what I read. I could, however, tell you about whatever insignificant thing I was daydreaming about as my eyes glanced at each of the words in the passage.

If the goal of reading the Bible is to tick a box so you can say you're a good Christian, then it's not too hard for me to do that. But if the goal of reading the Bible is to pay attention to what it's saying and hear from God as he speaks through it, then I have to admit that I struggle.

So I like to get help when I read the Bible. I often use books or apps to give me some other people's reflections on a passage because it helps me pay attention to what

I'm reading. Sometimes they have excellent, inspiring, and challenging things to say about the passage, and I get insights I would never have thought about on my own. Sometimes I think what they say is almost entirely wrong. But even disagreeing with someone makes me engage with the Bible and figure out why I think what they're saying is wrong.

People often ask me, 'Do you know any Bible devotions for youth?' I have one book that I always recommend and then I'm done.[1] This doesn't mean there aren't any good ones out there. I just haven't found them. So instead of searching every available teenage devotional to try to find the good ones, I thought I'd write some myself. I can't guarantee the devotions are good, but I can guarantee that they're here, in this book, and I wrote them. I'll let you be the judge of their quality.

WHY ARE THEY CALLED POP'S DEVOTIONS?

I didn't really want to call my series of devotions *Daily Wisdom from Pastor Tom French*, partly because no one calls me Pastor Tom French, but mostly because I don't enjoy naming things after myself.

Unlike me, my father, John French, is very good at spending time with God. In fact, he has done it almost every day since 1964. When I was growing up, I'd see him in the mornings reading his Bible and spending

---

1. If you're interested, that one book is *Best News Ever: Your 100-Day Guide to the Gospel of Mark* (Epsom: The Good Book Company, 2019) by my mate Chris Morphew. It's especially good if you're in year eight or below, but I read it and found it helpful and I'm at least three years out of high school.

Introduction to Pop's Devotions

time in prayer. Occasionally, I'd wake up at 5am to the sound of him singing hymns alone during his morning devotions. He showed me what it's like to spend time with God every day, so I thought, 'Who better to name my devotions after than my father?' His actual name isn't Pop, but his grandkids call him Pop – hence, Pop's Devotions!

HOW DOES THIS BOOK WORK?

I assume you could probably figure out how to read the devotions yourself, but if you're the kind of person who loves reading all the instructions, here are some ideas on how to use this book.

First, before you do anything, pray and ask that you would hear God as he speaks to you through his Word.

Now that you've prayed it's time to listen to God's Word. Each devotion is broken up into a few parts. On each day you get a passage of the Bible to read. So grab your Bible and read it. You can read it in a paper Bible, on an app, on a website, or listen to it read aloud. You may have noticed that there are lots of different translations of the Bible. I recommend the NIV, but there are plenty of good options out there. You will see that you repeat this reading over multiple days. This is because each day has a focus verse or verses, but these are only short, so to make sure you don't forget the context of what we're thinking about, I give you a longer passage to read. I promise reading the same passage a few days in a row will help you understand the book a lot better, and it won't take too long.

Next, I give you some things to consider. I have tried to give you some background information on the passage, and some ways it might make an impact in your life.

Remember, these are my thoughts on the passage. So if you read them and they're helpful, great! If you don't like them, that's okay – they aren't the Bible. I have tried to get things right, but I can make mistakes. So if your pastor or someone else who knows a lot about the Bible disagrees with me, that's okay too. It's an opportunity for you to do some further reading and praying and see what you think.

Following my thoughts, I give you a question to reflect on. It's important to consider how the Bible impacts you, so try to spend some time reflecting on the question.

Next, I suggest something you could do. I do this because the Bible should not just give us interesting things to think about; it should make a practical difference to how we live. If, after reading the passage, you find God is challenging you to do something else, fantastic! Do that! God's instructions are much more important than mine.

Finally, I give you a prayer to pray. Each prayer is just one or two sentences long, so use it as a springboard to help you begin your time of prayer with God. Tell God whatever you want. Tell him what you love about him, what you're thankful for, what you're sorry about, and what you'd love to see him do. He wants to hear from you, and I promise, once you start praying, you'll start seeing his answers all throughout your life. This is the amazing thing about our heavenly Father who is excited to be in relationship with us.

: Introduction to Pop's Devotions

GIVE YOURSELF A BREAK

My last piece of advice is this: give yourself a break. There are forty days of devotions in this book. If you're having a good time reading them every day, wonderful! However, if you're feeling the pressure to read them every day, or you miss a day or two (or more), no worries. There's nothing wrong with having a day off, spending time reading something else, or just spending time in prayer and reflection. Feel free to take fifty days, or sixty days, or seventy days to get through this book. God still loves you, even on the days you don't read your Bible. And he definitely doesn't love you more if you force yourself to do devotions every day. If you're spending more time with God because of Pop's Devotions (or any other devotions) than you normally would, then count it as a win.

Now, let me tell you a little about the book of the Bible we're going to study.

Introduction to Ephesians

Now, if you're anything like me when you get some new devotions, you don't want to read an introduction. Especially if you're sitting down, ready to do your devotion for the day, and then before you can begin Day One, there's a bunch of background information to read that you haven't budgeted the time for. If that's you, go do Day One. You can come back to this stuff later.

Why do I suggest you come back to this stuff? Because, though it's not absolutely vital, knowing some background information on the book you're about to spend the better part of six weeks in[2] will help you appreciate it more as you read it.

This is only going to be a brief introduction – some of you may wish I had gone into more depth. If that's you, I'd recommend having a look at the list of books in the Bibliography at the end of this book so you can find out more about Ephesians from people who are way smarter than me.

---

2. Or longer if, like most of people, you don't manage to read them every day.

WHO WROTE EPHESIANS?

If you read the first word of Ephesians you'll see that it tells us it was Paul who wrote it. For most of Church history, Ephesians was almost universally attributed to Paul. The problem is that in the last few hundred years, some Bible scholars have questioned that.

If you've read both Ephesians and Colossians, you may have noticed that they have a lot of similarities. Some people say this is because Paul wrote Colossians and then someone else, perhaps a devout disciple of Paul, copied bits of it to make a whole new letter in the style of Paul, then attributed it to Paul, and that's how we got Ephesians.[3]

The scholars who think this are basically saying, 'Ephesians is too similar to Colossians so it obviously couldn't have been written by Paul.' What's funny is that other times when scholars dispute the traditional authorship of a book by Paul they'll say, 'This book was not written by Paul because it's not similar enough to his other letters.' Poor Paul, he just can't catch a break.

I'm not sure the similarities between Ephesians and Colossians are a reason to dismiss Paul as the author. Have you ever had to write Christmas cards to a bunch of different people? There might be differences in your cards, but they have a lot of similarities, because you're trying to do the same thing in all your cards – you're wishing people a Merry Christmas. I think that's what's going on with Ephesians. Paul has similar things to say to the

---

3. In case you want a big word to pull out at parties with Bible nerds, writing a book in the name of someone else is known as *pseudepigrapha*. But if you do that these days it's usually not called pseudepigrapha, but fraud.

Introduction to Ephesians

Ephesians as he did to the Colossians, so the two books have a lot of parallels.

Aside from the Colossians controversy, there are also some scholars who think Ephesians isn't similar enough to Paul's other writings. They feel that the book of Ephesians doesn't fit with Paul's theology in his other letters. The letter, they say, is too future-oriented, and it focuses on the universal Church (every Christian) more than on a particular local church, like Paul does in books like 1 Corinthians or Galatians. The problem with this argument is that it reduces Paul to being a one-trick pony. As if he could not adjust his theological focus as the situation necessitated, or write something slightly different in style to his other writings. If that's the case, then he clearly isn't as talented as, say, C. S. Lewis, who wrote books on English literature and Christian theology, as well as children's and science fiction novels. For me, the arguments against Paul as the author of Ephesians don't stack up. Like people throughout most of Church history, I think Paul wrote it.

There is a lot we could say about who Paul was. But to make sure this introduction doesn't take up half the book, we'll cover a few things that might be helpful for understanding Ephesians. You can read the story of Paul (then known as Saul) in Acts; he was a religious extremist who hunted down Christians to have them imprisoned or killed, until he met the resurrected Jesus, who commissioned him to bring the good news of what Christ had done to those outside the Jewish faith. It was this commission to the Gentiles (non-Jews) that led him to start the church in Ephesus. It is also this emphasis in his message that we see reflected in Ephesians as he teaches about unity in the Church (Ephesians 2:19–22), some of which is brought about by Jesus making peace between Jews and Gentiles (2:11–18).

In Ephesians, we read that Paul is a 'prisoner for the Lord' (4:1). This is because he spent two years under house arrest in Rome, awaiting trial before Caesar. He had been accused by his enemies of committing crimes against the temple in Jerusalem, and for years he had been stuck in the Roman legal system while they sought to determine his fate. It was while in Rome that he wrote Ephesians, Philippians, Colossians, and Philemon. Having just spent two years at home in various stages of lockdown during the COVID-19 pandemic, I can say I'm sure it's God's provision that there were no video streaming services in Paul's day, or we may have ended up with fewer books in our Bibles.[4]

WHO WAS EPHESIANS WRITTEN TO?

In verse one of Ephesians, we're told that this letter is to 'the holy people in Ephesus'. You may think this clearly settles the question of who the book is written to. However, if you look carefully at your Bible, there is probably a little letter next to the word 'Ephesus'. At the bottom of the page (or after you tap on the letter, depending on how you read your Bible), you'll see a note that says something about how some early manuscripts don't have the words 'in Ephesus'. This is because there are a lot of different copies

---

4. To be fair to Paul, I assume he would have had the self-control to shut his YouTube tab and not to fire up Netflix when an epistle needed to be episted. (Episted isn't a real word, but it should be.)

Introduction to Ephesians

of the Bible out there, and some of the earliest versions of Ephesians don't state who the letter was sent to.[5]

Because the words 'in Ephesus' are missing from the earliest versions of the letter, and because, as we'll talk about soon, Ephesians doesn't seem to address particular issues in a particular church, many scholars think Paul wrote Ephesians for a group of churches around Ephesus. This means it was to be read out in a bunch of different churches in the Asia Minor region (which is where modern-day Turkey is). It was kind of like sending a mass email, if someone printed the email out and carried it from town to town so that each church could have a group reading. I think there is enough evidence that Ephesians was written for multiple churches so I'm on Team Circular Letter. As we go through these devotions, I'll be referring to the recipients as the churches of Ephesus or the Ephesian churches, acknowledging that even though the church in Ephesus was probably a recipient of the letter, it likely wasn't the only recipient.

That said, it is helpful to think about what Ephesus was like as a city because the culture there can teach us

---

5. Reading about missing words and differing copies of the Bible may lead you to ask, 'If we don't have a definitive copy of the Bible, how do we know it hasn't been changed over the years?' Let me answer the question with a question: how do you know that some copies of Ephesians don't have the words 'in Ephesus'? Because your Bible told you, so obviously, no one is hiding the fact that we don't have one perfect copy of the Bible. All the little differences that scholars have noticed or aren't totally sure about are listed for you to make up your own mind about. Of course, that's not the only reason you can trust that our version of the Bible is accurate, but I'm writing a footnote, not a chapter. If you want to find out more about this, try reading *Can I Really Trust the Bible?* by Barry Cooper (Epsom: The Good Book Company, 2014). It's really helpful, and it's also short, so it shouldn't take you too long to read.

a lot about what the Christian readers (or hearers) of 'Ephesians the letter' experienced in their day-to-day life.

Ephesus was one of the most important cities in the Roman Empire, often thought of as the capital of Asia Minor. It had a busy port and was a centre of trade, making it significant to the Roman economy. It was also a cultural centre, hosting athletic games and regularly holding festivals of music and theatre.

Ephesus was a centre for the worship of lots of gods and goddesses, particularly the goddess Artemis. She was the goddess of wild animals, the hunt, and childbirth. Ephesus had a temple of Artemis so impressive it was classified as one of the seven wonders of the ancient world. When worshipping Artemis, her followers would perform mystery rites. We know little about what happened during these ceremonies, but it is worth noting because the theme of 'mystery' plays a significant role in Paul's letter to the Ephesians. It's likely that when Paul wrote to the Ephesian churches about the revealed mystery of Christ, his readers' minds were drawn to the mystery rites associated with Artemis.

In Acts 19, we can read about Paul's action-packed visit to the city of Ephesus. There he taught in the synagogue and did heaps of healing and exorcisms. Paul was so successful in casting out evil spirits in Jesus' name that some Jewish exorcists thought they might also try invoking Jesus' name during their exorcisms. Unfortunately, it didn't go according to plan. Seven of them encountered a demon-possessed man, and after attempting to cast the demon out in Jesus' name, the evil spirit responded, 'Jesus I know, and Paul I know about, but who are you?' (Acts 19:15). The man then beat them up, causing them to flee naked and bleeding from the house (19:16). You know your ministry isn't going so well when you finish a pastoral visit running through the streets naked and covered in blood.

Because of events like this, respect for Jesus grew, and people who had put their trust in Jesus burned their scrolls of sorcery. So many scrolls were burned, their value was estimated to be 50,000 drachmas (v. 19), about $17 million in Australian currency. That's a lot of scrolls!

These Jesus-followers were causing significant economic disruption, so a silversmith who traded in shrines to Artemis met with his fellow workers and started a riot. While their exact demands were not clear (they just shouted 'Great is Artemis of the Ephesians' for a few hours (Acts 19:28, 34)), they clearly wanted Paul and his mates dealt with so they didn't lose their livelihood. After the riot, Paul said his last farewells and left Ephesus for Macedonia (Acts 20:1).

As you can see from these stories, Ephesus could be a pretty hairy place to live, especially for a Christian. All the magic, demons, and supernatural goings-on would have made an impression on the Ephesian churches. So as you read about Paul's discussion of the heavenly realms and Christ's victory over the powers of darkness, consider the significance his words would have had if you lived in a place like Ephesus. Having certainty of Christ's power would have been an immense encouragement when faced with the aggressive and spooky streets of Ephesus.

Ephesians

WHY WAS EPHESIANS WRITTEN?

When you read many of the letters in the New Testament, it's clear that Paul and the other apostles put pen to paper (or papyrus, actually) to address specific problems that had occurred in the churches. Thus, 1 Corinthians is really helpful if you're trying to figure out how to respond to a guy in your church who is sleeping with his stepmother. Ephesians isn't quite as specific. In Ephesians, it's difficult to pinpoint any particular problem in a local church that Paul might have been addressing. Instead, this letter contains general instruction in the Christian faith. One reason Ephesians is so loved by Christians today is its broad appeal. Because Paul wrote the letter to give general encouragement and instruction to a group of Christians, we can apply it in all sorts of situations in our own lives. It gives us some amazing foundations for what it means to be a Christian, who we are as Christians, and how we should live as a result of these wonderful truths.

When you read Ephesians, you'll notice that it is divided into two halves. Chapters 1–3 are mainly theology, while chapters 4–6 are much more practical. The first half is the theory, and the second half is about putting it into practice. Ephesians helps us readers see that the heady ideas about God's power, Christ's glory, the Spirit's unifying bond, and our predestination (to name just a few themes) not only make us feel good about being Christians but should have very real implications for how we live.

We know that the churches that received this letter were filled with both Jewish and Gentile believers, and one of the few specific issues that Paul addresses in the letter is how God has united Jews and Gentiles to each other by the work of Jesus. This unification is a defining characteristic of the Christian Church. While the churches of Ephesus lived in a world divided along racial, class, and gender lines, the church was to be a place that was unified under the lordship of Jesus. This unity in how Christians treated each other in their daily lives was to be a lived expression of the heavenly reality of their unity in Christ.

Paul also makes quite a few references to heavenly realms in his letter. This is not just heaven, but the spiritual realm where God, angels, Satan, demons, and other spiritual forces operate. Knowing about God's power in the heavenly realms and Christ's victory over evil can help us as Christians as we live our everyday lives. While we may believe in only what we see, it is important to remember there is a lot more going on than just what we can comprehend with our five senses. However, even in the supernatural realm, Jesus is in charge. For the ancient reader, especially those living in Ephesus, they would not have needed a reminder that the supernatural realm existed; that was a given for them. They needed to know that while the heavenly realms may seem contested, Jesus has been exalted 'far above all rule and authority, power and dominion, and every name that is invoked, not only in the present age but also in the one to come' (Ephesians 1:21). Because of his mighty power, the readers could put on their spiritual armour (6:10–18). If you're with Jesus, or 'in Christ' as Ephesians puts it, you're safe.

One last section worth mentioning is often referred to as the household code (5:21–6:9). This passage has instructions for wives and husbands, children and parents, and slaves and masters. There is a lot in this passage that is quite controversial today. As we'll see when we get to it (Days 34, 35, and 36), it was controversial then, too. What makes the passage worth mentioning here is that it shows how concerned Paul was that the gospel transforms not only how we see ourselves but also the relational power dynamics in our most foundational relationships. The gospel changes everything.

As we'll discover, Ephesians is a gold mine. It doesn't take too much work to see how what Paul wrote back then has application for us now. From Paul's overflowing prayers of praise to his reflections on Christ's salvation work, from his ethical commands to his instructions for a Spirit-filled life – all of it will bring us rich treasure if we take the time to dig into this letter and ask God to speak to us through it today.

DAY ONE
Everyone Loves Getting Letters

FOCUS VERSES: EPHESIANS 1:1–2

READ: Ephesians 1:1–14

SOME THINGS TO CONSIDER:
When I was in high school, I used to exchange letters with some friends from the local girls' school. These real, physical, pen-and-paper letters felt like the most exciting things ever. Girls were writing to me! They were giving me paper they'd written on with their actual female hands. After we'd exchanged our letters at the local train station on our way to our schools, I couldn't wait to read them. I'd devour them, hoping for any clues that they might be in love with me. Unfortunately, they were usually pretty dull discussions of what was going on during the class

they were ignoring as they wrote to me. Their letters would get passed around the classroom and I would get a brief message from all their friends. Once I had finished reading, I'd write a letter in response. Sometimes I'd also get my limited amount of school friends involved, too. The letters weren't very exciting, but at least they kept a lot of people entertained.

Ephesians is a letter. Like my letters, it was a community letter: one guy wrote it, but he wrote to a bunch of people. The book of Ephesians was an actual physical letter written by the apostle Paul, probably to a group a churches in the vicinity of the ancient city of Ephesus. Paul's letter was written to be passed around from church to church in the area so everyone could hear what he had to say. Paul's mate Tychicus was the postie. He had the job of delivering the letter to the churches and letting them know how Paul was doing (see Ephesians 6:21–22).

Paul begins the letter by introducing himself: 'Paul, an apostle of Christ Jesus by the will of God' (1:1).[6] You may know the story of Paul. He was a Jewish religious leader, intent on locking up and killing followers of Jesus as Christianity was just getting started. Then, one day, Jesus turned up and called him to change teams and start proclaiming what Jesus had done. (You can read the story in Acts 9.) Because of his encounter, Paul knew he had been sent by Jesus by God's design ('sent one' is what the

---

6. When Ephesians was written, it was often months between someone sending a letter and it being received. This is because people like Tychicus would deliver them after travelling over land and sea, by foot, boat, donkey, or horse. So I'm very pleased that Paul didn't start every one of his letters like I start most of my emails, 'Sorry for my slow reply...' His opening is much grander.

Day One: Everyone Loves Getting Letters

word apostle means). Paul didn't plan for his life to be about making Jesus known, that was all God's plan. Paul had, unwittingly, found himself in the exclusive group of first-generation apostles, those people who had seen the risen Jesus, and were called by him to help establish the new Christian Church.

Paul describes the people he was writing to as 'God's holy people', who are 'faithful in Christ Jesus' (1:1). As you read Ephesians, always remember that Paul was writing to a group of people. We can sometimes fall into the trap of thinking the Bible is God speaking directly to us as individuals. And while he does use the Bible to speak to us, we mustn't forget what the books of the Bible originally were – letters, histories, poetry, prophesies, and more. Ephesians was a letter intended to be read out to a group of Christians all together. As we follow Jesus, we're not meant to do it alone, we do it together. A lot of what Paul says in Ephesians is about what it means to be the Church – the people of God together – because following Jesus is a community affair.

In verse two, Paul proclaims grace and peace to those who are receiving the letter. This was Paul's standard way of opening a letter (it's more classy than 'Dear Valued Customer' or even my standard 'Hey!') but it also has some deep truth in it. Paul genuinely wanted his readers to experience peace and grace, which comes to them from God the Father because of the work of Jesus Christ. As we read this letter, we'll see the great news that God has saved us, and brought us into his family, because Jesus came to the world to rescue us from sin and death. Everything that

Paul says, even when instructing Christians on how to live, is powered by the great truth that we have received peace and grace from God.

Getting letters is exciting, but even better is when the contents of the letter live up to that excitement, and if these first two verses of Ephesians are anything to go by, this letter is a doozy! God has done incredible things for us – what they are, and how they change everything for us, is what the letter of Ephesians is all about.

SOMETHING TO REFLECT ON:
If you were to get a letter from God, what would you want him to say to you? You may like to write this down so you can revisit it when you finish reading Ephesians to see what God has said to you through this letter and how it relates.

SOMETHING TO DO:
As Ephesians was meant to be read by a group, do you have a friend or group of friends who you could read the letter with? Perhaps you could check in with each other every day to see what God is teaching them. Ask someone to join you in reading Ephesians – they can catch up, we're only two verses in!

A PRAYER TO PRAY:
Father God, thank you that you speak to me through your Word, the Bible. Help me hear and respond to what you are saying to me as I read about the great news of what Jesus has done, and how I might live because of it.

DAY TWO

Secret Billionaires

FOCUS VERSE: EPHESIANS 1:3

READ: Ephesians 1:1–14

SOME THINGS TO CONSIDER:
One day, I opened my bank account to find it had tens of thousands of dollars in it. For rich people, this may be what they find every day, but I am not rich people. I was 100 per cent sure that the day before my account only totalled a hundred dollars or less. I assumed that the bank had made some kind of mistake and I was going to have to give it back.

However, when I looked carefully at the transaction, I could see the money had come from my parents. So I asked them if they had mistakenly sent me a small fortune, and they told me there was no mistake. They were passing on some inheritance that I had received but which I had no idea was coming. This was very surprising, but certainly not unwelcome. Becoming instantly rich was, in fact, quite pleasant.

Verses 3–14 of Ephesians 1 are very surprising. In the Greek they were originally written in, these verses are one long sentence of praise that Paul pours out to God for all the amazing things he has done. The sentence has over two hundred words in it, which would probably get him terrible marks in an essay, but it seems like Paul was just too excited to pause for a full stop. As we read on, we'll see why.

Look at why Paul is praising God: because he has 'blessed us in the heavenly realms with every spiritual blessing in Christ' (1:3). It's easy to let your eyes skim over that sentence because it all just sounds very 'biblical'. But Paul is saying that those who are 'in Christ' (that's any Christian) have every spiritual blessing. That's like being a spiritual billionaire! If there is something good that is available for you in the heavenly realms, it's yours, because you're in Christ.

'Ahh, yes, but there's the catch!' you may be thinking. 'We're rich in the heavenly realms, not on earth. What even are the heavenly realms?' Well, I'm glad I pretended you asked. The 'heavenly realms' is a phrase that only occurs in Ephesians, but it's an important one.

We live in a world that we can see, hear, smell, taste, and touch, and we may be tempted to believe that this physical reality is the most important one. However, the Bible lets us in on a whole greater reality, the reality we cannot physically sense but is there nonetheless – the reality of angels and demons, where God rules on his throne, and where Jesus is eternally worshipped. The realm where the spiritual life is played out across the universe and beyond – that is the heavenly realms. We may think of heaven as some faraway place where we go when we die, but there is so much more going on. The heavenly realms are in heaven, where the Father and the Son are, but it's also here on earth, where the Holy Spirit is, and where good and bad spiritual forces are at work. You may not feel it, but you exist as much in the heavenly realms as you do in the physical ones. And it's in that reality that you and I, and all who are in Christ, have every single spiritual blessing. Isn't that surprising? It's even better than opening your bank account to find unexpected thousands.

Many of the stories we love to read in books and watch in movies are about an ordinary person who discovers one day that they have superpowers, or are royalty in a faraway kingdom, or they can talk to animals, or something similar. Those things are all great, but they aren't real. When we read the true story of Jesus, we see a man who may not have looked all that impressive – an average, working-class carpenter – but was in fact the cosmic King, on a mission to rescue the entire universe from the powers of darkness. And now you and I, if we've put our trust in Jesus, are part of that story, on the side of the good guys, receiving every spiritual blessing available to us because Jesus has made us his. That's not a fantasy, that's reality, whether or not you can see it.

Tomorrow we're going to begin digging into what exactly these spiritual blessings are, but for now, it might be worth joining with Paul to praise God for every good thing he has given us in his Son.

SOMETHING TO REFLECT ON:
How might knowing that in the heavenly realms you have every spiritual blessing in Christ change your life and your experience of the physical world?

SOMETHING TO DO:
Spend some time praising God for everything you can think of that he has given us and done for us in Jesus.

A PRAYER TO PRAY:
Praise be to the God and Father of our Lord Jesus Christ, who has blessed us in the heavenly realms with every spiritual blessing in Christ.

DAY THREE

Chosen Before Time

FOCUS VERSES: EPHESIANS 1:4–6

READ: Ephesians 1:1–14

SOME THINGS TO CONSIDER:
As I write this, my wife is pregnant with our first child. By the time you read this, I hope the baby will be born, and we'll have met them. I currently know little about them: I know they exist; I know they have limbs; and I know they can kick my wife in the ribs with those limbs (a habit I hope they'll stop after the birth). The first time we knew the baby existed was a few weeks after the baby was conceived. For a little while, there wasn't a single person on earth who knew about the little life that was growing in my wife's womb. But from the moment we knew about the baby, we were excited to meet them

and we had plans to love them as best we could. They don't know yet that we know about them and love them, but one day they will.

In today's verses, Paul lets us in on the first of the spiritual blessings we were talking about yesterday. He tells us that before we existed, before even the earth existed, God knew about us, loved us, and had chosen us to be 'holy and blameless' and to become part of his family. That is mind-boggling!

You may read the word 'predestined' in verse 5 and be a little confused. Predestination is the idea that God made a plan, before the beginning of time, for us to be saved. He has chosen us to choose him. The problem then comes when we say, 'Hold on, didn't I choose God? If God chose me before I existed, how can I have chosen him?' So did God choose you or did you choose God? The answer to the question is 'yes'. God chose you and you chose God. The Bible clearly teaches us that God chose us before he had even begun making the world, and the Bible also clearly teaches human responsibility, and the need for us to respond to God in repentance and faith.

Over the years, many people smarter than me have tried to solve this contradiction. I don't have time to go into the whole thing now, but I don't think the issue of predestination is a problem to be solved.[7] In God, two contradictory things can be true at the same time. The

---

[7]. If you really want me to explain my ideas about predestination to you, I made a low-quality video about it for my YouTube channel. Head to youtube.com/twfrench and search for 'Predestination'. If you've read other books of mine, you'll know this YouTube video has saved me a lot of typing about predestination over the years.

Day Three: Chosen Before Time

Bible is full of these paradoxes. How can Jesus be fully God and fully man at the same time? I don't know, but he is. How can God be three persons and one God? I can't understand it, but the Bible teaches it. Just because our minds can't solve a conundrum, doesn't mean it's unsolvable in the infinite power and wisdom of God. We have to live with the tension that both things can be true, and trust God to figure out how it works.

If all this hurts your brain, remember that the point of knowing about predestination is not to stress us out, but to be a blessing! How does it feel to know that before God had created any human, he knew you, loved you, and had chosen you to be adopted into his family? Incredible, right?

My little sister is adopted, but she isn't a second-class child in our family. She's just as loved by my parents and just as much a part of my family as my older sister and me. When we're adopted into God's family, we are adopted in to 'sonship' (1:5). Sonship, because in ancient families sons had full rights in a family while daughters only got some rights. It's sexist, I know, but here Paul is being the opposite of sexist. He's telling us that whether female or male, all of us are adopted into 'sonship' – full rights – in God's family when we trust in Jesus.

If we're adopted then who is God's natural-born child? Jesus. So we get the same family blessings that Jesus does. Amazing!

We aren't just chosen to become part of the family and then forgotten, we're chosen so that we might be 'holy and blameless in his sight' (1:4). You may not feel holy or blameless, but Jesus is, and because he took your place when he died for you, you receive his holiness and blamelessness as your own. And as you do this, slowly but surely God transforms you, so your life and behaviour reflects your status.

Why does God do all this? Not because anyone forces him to, but because he wants to – it is all 'freely given us in the One he loves' (1:6), that's Jesus. And all of it is to the 'praise of his glorious grace' – he does it so that all creation, in the earthly and heavenly realms, might know and marvel at his love towards us. As we understand what he has done for us, how can we not?

SOMETHING TO REFLECT ON:
How does it feel to know that God chose you to be part of his family before he created the world? What does that do for your sense of how much he loves you?

SOMETHING TO DO:
When you are tempted to talk down to yourself, remind yourself that you are God's adopted child, and that he chose you before the beginning of time. You might not always get things right, but nothing can take away your status before God.

A PRAYER TO PRAY:
God beyond all time, thank you that before the earth existed, you knew me and loved me. Help me live a life that reflects your love, and help me live out my calling to be holy and blameless.

DAY FOUR

'Here's the Plan...'

FOCUS VERSES: EPHESIANS 1:7–10

READ: Ephesians 1:1–14

SOME THINGS TO CONSIDER:
If you hear the word 'redemption', what do you think of? Redeeming discount codes? People who did bad things, but seek redemption by turning their life around? A series of movies that has become progressively worse, but is redeemed when an excellent new instalment comes out?

As Paul continues to describe some of our spiritual blessings in Christ, he uses the word 'redemption'. In Ephesians, it has a different, but related, meaning to the examples above. The word is about the price paid to free a slave from slavery. There is still the idea of handing something over in order to receive something (like with the discount code), and of a situation getting turned around (like with the bad people, and the movie franchise), but the biblical word helps us to better understand what Jesus has done for us. We didn't redeem ourselves. We were in slavery to sin and death, but we have redemption through Jesus' blood. When Jesus died on the cross, he was paying the price to set us free from our sin. Instead of us having to make a payment, Jesus purchased our forgiveness.

Next, we're told that this is 'in accordance with the riches of God's grace that he lavished on us' (1:7–8). The word lavished is an excellent word. I heard a friend speak about it once in a Bible talk. As she was speaking, she pulled out a piece of bread and some chocolate spread. She put a small amount of the spread on the bread and asked if we thought she had lavished it on? Of course she hadn't. She put a bit more on – the amount your mum might allow you to have on the bread. Still she hadn't lavished it on. She put a lot more on – the amount I might put on my own piece of bread. Still not lavished. She ended up dumping the entire container out so the spread had covered the bread, was all over her hand, up her arm, and falling on the floor. 'Now that's lavished on,' she pronounced. Whenever I read the word lavished in the Bible, I think of my friend's talk, because God is not a stingy God. When Jesus gave his life for you, he wasn't doing it grudgingly, and he didn't do the bare minimum. God's redemption of us comes out of his abundant supply of grace for us that is more than we need and will never run out.

Day Four: 'Here's the Plan...'

That's amazing, but you want to know another blessing that we have in Christ? We've been let in on the mystery of God's will. There is often a scene in movies, about two-thirds of the way through, where the hero makes a plan. Inevitably, they'll gather all their friends and sidekicks around them and say, 'Alright, this is what we're going to do...' and then the scene will cut away because we the audience aren't allowed to know the plan, it remains a mystery to us, otherwise the climax of the film would be ruined. You can be sure in movies that if you get told the plan beforehand, it's going to go wrong, leaving you unsure of how the hero will succeed. If you don't get told the plan, it's probably going to go right, even though you think things have gone wrong.

Well, God has let us in on the mystery of what he's up to in the universe. The plan is this: at exactly the right time, everything in all the universe, both the spiritual and physical, the visible and invisible, is going to be brought to unity in Jesus. That means that there will be nothing that is not how Jesus intends it. There will be no more rebellion against God, no more sin and suffering, no more cancer, mental illness, war, or deadly volcanos.[8] All of God's creation is going to be renewed and at the centre of it all will be Jesus Christ, the gracious King who gave his life to redeem the world, and now lives forever.

According to the rules of movies, because we know the plan there will be complications and the plan

---

8. I wouldn't want to say there will be no more volcanos at all, because volcanos that don't kill people or cause massive devastation are kind of awesome. Imagine getting to watch a volcano blow up knowing it's completely safe. It'd be like fireworks but at least thirty times more amazing!

may not succeed. Looking at yourself, or the world, you may feel that there is no way God can or will set all this right. But we know the lengths God has gone to to redeem us, we know the grace he has lavished on us, and we know Jesus rose from the dead, so we can be sure God is going to get it done. The mystery has been revealed to us, now we get to wait and see how it unfolds.

SOMETHING TO REFLECT ON:
When are you most likely to doubt that God has the future safely in his hands? How can you remind yourself of Jesus' victory over sin and death at the cross when you are doubting God's control over the future?

SOMETHING TO DO:
Write down all your fears about your future, and all the sins that you continue to feel guilty for. Give them to God in prayer, knowing that he has lavished his grace on you, forgiven your sins, and has your future safe in his hands.

A PRAYER TO PRAY:
Gracious God, thank you that you have lavished your grace upon me so that I might be forgiven. Help me to trust that with the same love that you redeemed your people, you are making the future and all reality right in Jesus.

DAY FIVE

No Second-class Citizens

FOCUS VERSES: EPHESIANS 1:11–14

READ: Ephesians 1:1–14

SOME THINGS TO CONSIDER:
I love flying in planes. When there isn't a raging global pandemic, I get to do quite a lot of flying. On these flights, I'm always sitting up the back of the plane in the cheap seats, but I love it nonetheless. As I walk down the aisle, I see the people in business class with the fancy seats and yummy meals, and I wish I could join them. In fact, one day I did join the elite few up the front of the plane. I had a lot of frequent flyer points, and my wife and I were going on our first flight in almost a year (because of that pesky, raging, global pandemic) so I treated us to a free business

class flight. I was finally in the cool group on the plane. The airline welcomed us in to their swanky lounge before our flight, on the plane we got to sit in the oversized seats (the buttons to control them are very confusing), we got a fancy meal to eat during the flight, and we got to listen to the things posh people complain about as we sat among our fellow business class passengers.[9] Would I fly business class again? Not if I have to pay for it. The tickets are five times more expensive – it's definitely not worth that.

I'm not here to give a review of business class flights (I wish that were my job though, how fun!). I tell you about that experience because there are a lot of situations in life where there is an in-group and an out-group. There is a group that seem to get all the perks, and then there is everyone else.

You could be forgiven for thinking that's how things worked with God's people, the Jews. They were people chosen by God. They got the inside track on salvation. They got to hear about Jesus' saving work and put their trust in him. And then there was everyone else. But Paul is saying in today's verses that this isn't actually the case. There are the Jews, and they were chosen by God to be 'the first to put [their] hope in Christ' (1:12), which is a very special privilege. But what about everyone else; all those people who aren't Jewish (that is, the Gentiles)? Paul reminds them that: 'you also were included in Christ when you heard the message of truth, the gospel of your salvation' (1:13). Everyone has

---

9. They were complaining that the business class lounge closed before the flight left and they had to sit in the normal airport lounge like the commoners. (They didn't say 'commoners', I added that in.)

Day Five: No Second-class Citizens

the opportunity now to be in the 'in-group' – business class is open to all. Alright, it's better than business class!

One of the many spiritual blessings of being in Christ is that everyone, no matter what their background or heritage, is welcome in God's family.

And how can we be sure of that? Because we have the Holy Spirit. There are a lot of amazing things that the Holy Spirit does for us and one of those things is being 'a seal' (1:13). Not a seal that eats fish (though I guess the Holy Spirit could do that too if he wanted), but a seal like a mark that someone would put on something to show it belonged to them. Like when you see the seal of the President of the United States on a podium, you know that's their podium, which they will speak at. The Holy Spirit living in every Christian, Jew or Gentile, lets us know we belong to God.

The Holy Spirit 'is a deposit guaranteeing our inheritance until the redemption of those who are God's possession' (1:14). When I was a kid, I saw a hoodie in the shops that I really wanted because it was a brand everyone at school told me was cool. My mum didn't want to buy it for me because it was stupidly expensive. But she did let me put it on lay-by so that I could pay it off in instalments. This meant we paid a deposit to the store and they put the hoodie aside with my name on it (like my seal perhaps?). Then each week for a couple of months, I came back to pay off a little more of the hoodie, till I finally paid the whole price and I got to take the hoodie home. I wore that hoodie proudly for at least a month until I lost it.

The Holy Spirit is a deposit, promising us that God will not forget about us or reject us. Just like that hoodie was mine, we are his. If we are saved by Jesus, God has given us the Holy Spirit to live in us, and to be a constant reminder that God will never leave us and he's coming back for us. One day we will get to live with him forever in the new creation, all first-class citizens of God's perfect society.

SOMETHING TO REFLECT ON:
Have you ever felt like you were in an 'out-group'? What does it mean to you that, with Jesus, everyone is welcome and no one is second-class?

SOMETHING TO DO:
Look back through Ephesians 1:1–14 and make a note of every spiritual blessing that Paul has listed. Take some time to thank God for them, knowing that God has given you every spiritual blessing in Christ.

A PRAYER TO PRAY:
Generous God, I praise you for giving me so much in Christ. Help me always to know your presence in me by your Holy Spirit. Help me look forward to the time when Jesus will come back for me, and all his people, as he puts the world right.

DAY SIX

The Menu

FOCUS VERSES: EPHESIANS 1:15–19A

READ: Ephesians 1:15–23

SOME THINGS TO CONSIDER:
Have you ever been to a restaurant with someone and they've said, 'Order anything you want on the menu. I'm paying!' What did you do? Are you the person who orders the most expensive thing because when else will you get the chance to taste the best food on someone else's coin? Did you order the cheapest thing so they didn't think you were taking advantage of them? Or did you order something mid-ranged so that they weren't offended that you were taking advantage of them, or offended that you weren't accepting their generosity?

The social etiquette of ordering when someone else is paying can be tough. What about when you're asking God for something? Should you ask for the most extravagant thing you can think of? (Lord, give me great abs and a private jet! Amen.) Should you just ask for small things he is likely to answer? (Lord, it's Wednesday today. Please make tomorrow Thursday. Amen.) Should you find some middle ground?

In today's passage, we see Paul praying for the church, and what he asks for can teach us something about how we can pray. He doesn't hold back his requests, but he also doesn't ask for what we might expect him to. Paul doesn't ask God to heal sick people in the congregation, or to take away any persecution they might face for their faith, and he definitely doesn't pray that they will be wealthy. He asks for one big thing: that the people might know God better.

I can imagine if you were hearing Ephesians for the first time and you found out Paul, a spiritual giant, was praying for you, you would be excited. But then when you found out he asked that you might know God better, you would be pretty disappointed. Especially when there were so many more practical things Paul could have asked for.

But perhaps Paul knew exactly what he was doing. In the passage, Paul explains what he wants the church to know about God. To know the hope to which they were called (1:18), the riches of their inheritance (1:18), and God's power for believers (1:19).

Understanding 'the hope to which he has called [them]' is about knowing deep in their truest selves what

Day Six: The Menu

happened when they were saved. This is a knowledge about their past. Knowing 'the hope' means knowing that not only have they been forgiven for their sins but they have become part of God's family; they are taking part in the new creation, and one day they will rise again just like Jesus!

The 'riches of [their] inheritance' is about their future. When the Bible talks about God's inheritance it is not always clear if it's the inheritance God gets from us, or the inheritance we get from God. The fact that God will never die might make it seem like we would just be eternally waiting for something. But what if when we die we get God, and he gets us? We are his inheritance, we are his treasure, and he becomes ours. He is holding nothing back from us. The future is bright!

The last knowledge is about the present, God's 'incomparably great power for us who believe'. In Ephesus, power was a big deal. There were shrines to the god Artemis, whom people would pray to seeking blessing and spiritual power. Many of the people who became Christians in Ephesus had also practiced the magic arts – a way of harnessing spiritual power for yourself. So when Paul prayed that the churches might know God's incomparably great power, he was asking that the Christians would know that what was available to them each day was infinitely more potent than anything they had practiced, or anyone they had prayed to, before. (We'll think more about this power tomorrow.)

Paul understood that when a Christian knows God, and what he has done for us, it can transform our lives. It's more important that we understand what we already have rather than asking for more stuff. If we truly knew what being saved by Jesus has done for our past, our future, and our present, we wouldn't feel like we needed more of anything. We could face sickness, loneliness, bullying, persecution, and all our other hardships with the transformed perspective and power of people who truly know God. That's not just ordering the best thing on the menu, that's having the chef as your dad, and getting the very best meal every time.

When you pray, it's okay to ask God for anything that you think he might want for you and the people around you. It's good to ask him for simple things like material needs. After all, Jesus taught us to pray and ask for our daily bread (Matthew 6:11). But don't forget to order big off the menu too – ask that you might know God. Knowing God changes everything.

SOMETHING TO REFLECT ON:
When was the last time you prayed that you might gain a deeper knowledge of God?

SOMETHING TO DO:
Spend some time in prayer for yourself and for those who you know, that you all would know God better.

A PRAYER TO PRAY:
Father God, please give me the desire to know you, and for the Spirit of revelation, that my understanding of you might grow more and more. Help me seek the same wonderful knowledge for my friends, family, and those around me, too.

DAY SEVEN
Friends in High Places

FOCUS VERSES: EPHESIANS 1:19B-21

READ: Ephesians 1:15–23

SOME THINGS TO CONSIDER:
Who is the most powerful person you know? I know someone, who knows someone, who knows someone, who knows the King of England. So I'm pretty much best friends with His Majesty. I don't know how much power the King actually has, but I think if he really wanted to, he could dismiss the entire government of Australia, so that's pretty powerful. Maybe if one day I have a problem with the government I can ask my friend, to ask their friend, to ask their friend, to ask Charlie to dissolve the parliament. I'm sure he'd listen to me.

It's clear that I'm not a powerful person in the big scheme of things, unless you consider what Paul said yesterday, that there is 'incomparably great power for us who believe' (1:19). Today we see what that power is. It is 'the same as the mighty strength [God] exerted when he raised Christ from the dead and seated him at his right hand in the heavenly realms' (1:19–20). When you think about it, that's a lot of power!

Where I live, people under sixteen aren't allowed to drive a car, and people under eighteen aren't allowed to vote. As a society, we've decided it's too much power for them. But if you're a young Christian you have much more power available to you than a licence or a chance to vote. You have the same power that raised Jesus from the dead! How can you access it? Through prayer and faithfulness. That means asking God for what we need (prayer) and then living the way he calls us to, trusting that he will provide (faithfulness).

Sometimes people think that when they want God to do something, they need to pray a special prayer, or not eat food, or anoint something with holy oil. While ways of praying, fasting, and anointing are all taught in the Bible, and can be helpful, if we're not careful they can take on the flavour of a magic spell, used to coerce God into doing what we want him to do.

Prayer is about accessing your relationship with God. Look at Paul's description of Jesus in verse 21. Now that he is risen from the dead, and ascended into the heavenly realms, his position and power is entirely unmatched by any human or spiritual power, now and

Day Seven: Friends in High Places

forever. This is the relationship you are entering in to in prayer.

Paul writes that Jesus' name is far above any name that is invoked. In Paul's day, people would invoke the name of their gods in prayer and magic rituals to access spiritual power in their lives. In Western cultures, we're more likely to invoke the name of earthly authorities (e.g. the King) to get stuff done, or even our own name, or the human or consumer rights that we feel belong to us. But the name of a god, a political figure, a billionaire, or even your own name, has nothing on the authority and power that is behind the name of Jesus.

As we pray and live a faithful life, we will see God's power at work in our lives. Perhaps not to call down lightning on our enemies, or turn a loaf of bread into gold, but to become more like Jesus, to defeat evil in our lives, to share the good news of Jesus with those around us, and to love people who are difficult to love. The power of Jesus turns lives upside down, setting us free from guilt and shame, and empowering us to live for God. Sometimes God answers our prayers in physically miraculous ways, healing or provision, but God is always at work bringing his power to bear in the lives of believers. If we're willing to keep our eyes open, we'll see and experience God's incomparably great power for us who believe.

SOMETHING TO REFLECT ON:
If you truly believed that Jesus is all-powerful, and his power if available for you, how would this change how you lived?

SOMETHING TO DO:
What is one thing you can do because you trust in the power of Jesus? Perhaps it's inviting a friend to read the Bible with you? Maybe it's taking courageous steps to defeat a recurring sin in your life? Could it be forgiving someone who has hurt you? Do one faithful thing today because you trust in the power of Jesus.

A PRAYER TO PRAY:
Almighty God, thank you for your power for me. Help me know your power and to trust in it, as I seek to live for you.

DAY EIGHT

The Fullness

FOCUS VERSES: EPHESIANS 1:22–23

READ: Ephesians 1:1–23

SOME THINGS TO CONSIDER:
Every now and again you find out something very surprising about someone you know. Like when you discover your friend's mum is the CEO of a huge, billion-dollar company, or when you learn that the quiet kid at youth group is actually a black belt in some deadly martial art and could snap your neck easily, or when you find out that one of my front teeth is fake. (Maybe that last one isn't as good as the first two.) What's perhaps more surprising than all of that is when you find out something impressive you didn't know about yourself. If you're a Christian, today's passage might do just that.

In verse 22, Paul moves from telling us about Jesus' all-encompassing power and authority to his role as head of the Church. This means Jesus is both the head of your local church which you might attend each Sunday and the head of the universal Church – that is all the people who believe in Jesus, they are 'the Church'. In both senses, after having all things put under his feet, being head of the Church seems rather trivial. It's like saying, 'Dr Winifred Winner has three PhDs as well as being a trained medical doctor. She has twenty-two Olympic gold medals in six different sports, she was Australia's youngest ever prime minister, she once single-handedly defeated twelve terrorists who were holding 100 people hostage in a bank vault, and she also has a very good toothbrush.' The Church, compared to all the many things over which Jesus rules, feels about as significant as his toothbrush. I mean, have you been to church lately? We're a bunch of bumbling, sinful people, who gather every week to sing soft-rock ballads to God, then attempt to stay awake through a twenty-minute or longer monologue on the greatest book ever written – which we still manage to make boring. We don't seem significant enough to get much of a mention in the list of Jesus' magnificent feats and jurisdictions.

What's more, not only is Jesus the head of the Church, in that he's in charge, but we also see that the Church is his body! If I were Jesus I'd pick a better body. He could have an amazing Holy Spirit-powered mech-warrior to be his body, but he chooses the Church.

Day Eight: The Fullness

Of course, the Church is not Jesus' actual body. He still has his actual physical body in heaven. But the Church is Jesus' physical presence on earth. We Christians are how Jesus gets most of his work done in the world.

In fact, we're told that the Church is 'the fullness of him who fills everything in every way' (1:23). How can we be Jesus' fullness? To be honest, Bible scholars have spent a lot of time trying to understand what this verse means. I think it probably means that if Jesus is the ruler of all the universe, he has a special 'filling' for his people, the Church. Not that Jesus is less without the Church, but the Church is nothing without the fullness of Jesus. The Holy Spirit has taken up residence in God's people, and it's through the Church that Jesus is bringing glory to himself. Jesus has a very special work to do through the Church. That he has saved us and is changing us is part of the fullness of Jesus. The stories of people coming to faith in him through the work of the Church are part of the fullness of Jesus. The work to love those who are hurting and marginalised, and to bring justice to this world, is part of the fullness of Jesus.

If you're a Christian, none of this should give you a big head. We're only significant because Jesus makes us significant; without Jesus choosing to fill us with his fullness, we're nothing. But what it should do for us is give us joy that we get to be the means through which Jesus achieves his earthly mission. Plus, it should encourage us to take church seriously, not just what we do together on a Sunday (though that is part of it), but everything we do together as the people of God. We're the fullness of Christ on mission as his body, bringing Jesus' presence to a world who needs to know him. That's pretty surprising for a people as unimpressive as us.

SOMETHING TO REFLECT ON:
How do you view the people of God? Considering this passage, how should your view change?

SOMETHING TO DO:
As you go about your day today, remind yourself that, along with all the other Christians you know, you're on mission for Jesus. Let that change how you live, knowing that you are part of his body here on earth.

A PRAYER TO PRAY:
God of the universe, thank you that we get the privilege of being part of Christ's body. Help me take my role seriously. Help me appreciate and praise you for how Jesus is at work through the Church, which is the fullness of Christ.

DAY NINE

Diagnosis: Death

FOCUS VERSES: EPHESIANS 2:1–3

READ: Ephesians 2:1–10

SOME THINGS TO CONSIDER:
I hadn't been feeling too well recently. So the doctor sent me to get some tests done to make sure there was nothing wrong with me. The doctor thought there was nothing wrong with me. I thought there was nothing wrong with me. But just to make sure, we got some tests done. As I waited for the results, I tried not to imagine all the terrible diseases I could be dying of. When I entered the doctor's office, my heart was beating fast, my underarms were sweating, and I couldn't quite speak properly. The doctor sat me down and told me that everything looked good. I wasn't dying any quicker than anyone else. My

Ephesians

symptoms were probably stemming from my anxiety, which, it seems, hadn't been helped by my wondering if I was dying. Finding out that I was okay turned out to be great for my anxiety! Apart from telling me to come back if it got worse, he also suggested that I eat less animal fat and do a bit more exercise, because he's a doctor and has to say that. Phew! Everything was okay!

Imagine, however, if I had gone to the doctor and he said, 'Oh, you're doing great now, but before... My test results show that sometime in the past you were dead.' That would be very strange. As far as I know, I've been alive my entire life. But when we read our focus verses for today, we can see that Paul begs to differ. If you're a Christian, before you put your trust in Jesus, you were dead. If you're not a Christian, then I'm sad to say, you're dead right now.[10]

'How can that be?' you may ask. 'I have no memory of being dead. And the non-Christians I know eat, drink, laugh, and look very much alive.' What Paul is talking about here is being spiritually dead. Physically, everything might have been going just fine before we met Jesus, but because of our 'transgressions and sins' (2:1) we were dead.[11] We had no future, no way of saving ourselves, and a spiritual ECG would have found no heartbeat.

---

10. But isn't it great you're reading Ephesians – it's got all the information you need to be made alive!
11. Transgressions are the things we actively do wrong, like stealing. Sins are where we fall short of God's standard, like failing to do what we know is right, like speaking up for someone who is being treated badly. Together, transgressions and sins cover all our rebellion against God, the bad things we do, and the good we fail to do.

Day Nine: Diagnosis: Death

What does this dead life look like? Paul says that it's a life characterised by following three things: the world, the devil, and our desires.[12]

The world, because instead of having our life shaped by the attitudes of God, it is shaped by the prevailing wisdom and culture of the people we live among. The devil, because there is an evil, spiritual being, who hates God and is doing his best to tempt us into rebellion against him. And our desires, or the 'cravings of our flesh' (2:3), because we've given in to our appetites, even if they're not good for us. People often think of the 'cravings of the flesh' as being all about sex, drugs, and alcohol (which they can be), but we also crave recognition, comfort, power, fame, wealth, influence, and more. All these cravings, if not directed towards God-honouring pursuits, lead us into sin and death.

The result of all this is that we were 'by nature deserving of wrath' (2:3). This might seem pretty harsh, and we don't really like the idea of God punishing sin, especially when we're just living out our God-given desires.[13] But God's wrath is not about arbitrary

---

12. You may have heard people talking about 'the world, the flesh, and the devil'. This is what they're talking about.
13. You may wonder how all desires can be God-given. For example, if someone is obsessed with power, how is that God-given? Or someone is full of lust, how is that God-given? I think our 'cravings of the flesh' are expressions of our godly desires for God's good gifts that have gone wrong. The desire for power can come from the godly desire to effect change for good in the world. Adam and Eve were given power by God to rule the world in his place. Jesus uses his power to serve others. Power is a good gift from God, but we often want it for ourselves to rule over others and make our own lives better. This is a sinful expression of a good thing. Lust is an expression of our desire for sexual and relational intimacy, which is

punishment, or him being a bit of a loose unit who could fly off the handle at any moment. God's wrath is about dealing properly with evil. All the worst things in the world, from lies and malicious gossip, to genocide and war crimes, come from humanity's impulse to follow the world, the devil, and our desires. For God not to respond with wrath against everything terrible that has been done, would make him a God who didn't care. He would turn a blind eye to all the pain and suffering in the world, including your pain and suffering and that of those you love, which has come about because of others' transgressions and sins. God's wrath is not the opposite of his love, it is a necessary part of it. Without wrath, justice is never done, and evil wins.

Even so, as people dead in our transgressions and sins, there was no hope for us as we faced the wrath of God. Dead people couldn't redeem themselves even if they wanted to – they're dead. Which is all pretty depressing if verse 3 was the end of what Paul had to say to us. However, the first word of verse 4 is 'But...' 'But' means it's not the end of the story. 'But' means there is hope. We'll get to that tomorrow. (Spoiler alert, it's got something to do with Jesus.) For now, we can remember what our situation was once like. And we can thank God that even a diagnosis of death is not the end of the story.

---

a good gift from God (which was also given to Adam and Eve at creation). But it becomes sinful when it is indulged outside of a loving marriage, and is used to exploit and dehumanise others.

SOMETHING TO REFLECT ON:
How does the diagnosis of death affect how you consider your sin? Do you view it as seriously as God?

SOMETHING TO DO:
Spend some time examining your life to see how you may have given in to the world, the devil, and your desires. Thank God that he has rescued you, and is helping you now live for him.

A PRAYER TO PRAY:
God of love, thank you that while my transgressions and sins brought me death, you have not left me dead. Help me understand your wrath, so that I might understand your love better and what you have rescued me from.

DAY TEN

The Cliffhanger

FOCUS VERSES: EPHESIANS 2:4–7

READ: Ephesians 2:1–10

SOME THINGS TO CONSIDER:
I hate it when TV shows finish an episode on a cliffhanger, only to have some super simple resolution in the first ten seconds of the next episode. Like a masked man might jump out in front of the main character with a gun and say, 'You're dead this time, McGrey,' and then the credits will roll. I'll spend a whole week (assuming I can't stream the whole season) wondering if McGrey will be alright, when at the beginning of the next episode, the villain will rip off their mask and it will just be McGrey's brother pulling a prank. It's the worst. I much prefer a cliffhanger where there are real consequences for the story.

Ephesians

Remember yesterday how we finished on that cliffhanger where we were all dead, deserving of wrath, and with no hope of being made alive again? Today we see the hero who has saved us, and it's not some underwhelming resolution. It's the greatest redemption story in history.[14]

Everything turns around with that small word at the beginning of verse 4: 'But...' It is the signifier that everything is changing. We were all dead, and dead people can't do anything for themselves, but along comes our rescuer. 'But because of his great love for us, God, who is rich in mercy...' (2:4). Paul is telling us a few things in this first sentence: Our rescuer is God. His character is 'rich in mercy', which means he does not give people the wrath they deserve. His reason for saving us is 'because of his great love for us'; he didn't save us because we impressed him, or because we have something he needs. No, we can receive his mercy, only because he loves us.

And what does his mercy look like? He 'made us alive with Christ' (2:5). We may have been dead, but just as Jesus has been made alive, so have we. Our spiritual death has been reversed. And this isn't just any old revivification, we have been raised up with Christ and seated with him in the heavenly realms (2:6)! Remember how in chapter 1 Paul kept talking about how we are 'in Christ'? Now we see that we are so much 'in Christ' that his resurrection is our resurrection, and his seat in

---

14. Admittedly, there wasn't really a cliffhanger. If you have been reading the full reading each day, you'd know what happened. I just decided to split the devotions there. But all cliffhangers are artificial story devices anyway, so why not put one in our Bible reading if we want to?

Day Ten: The Cliffhanger

heaven is also ours! This boggles the mind! Even though you're sitting wherever you are right now (I assume you're sitting, but I guess you could also be standing, lying down, or floating in a lake), you are also sitting in heaven with Jesus. This isn't just that Jesus has saved a place for you, you're already sitting there. Notice that Paul says that Jesus 'seated us with him'. It's past tense, we're already there. I don't quite know how this works, it's a mystery to me, but isn't it amazing to know that, while God may not have finished with you, making you into the person he wants you to be, he has already raised you up with Jesus? He's not waiting to see how you'll turn out and if his investment in you is worth it. You were dead, but now you've been raised up to eternal life. In a very real way, you're already at home with Jesus!

Why would God do all this? 'In order that in the coming ages he might show the incomparable riches of his grace, expressed in his kindness to us in Christ Jesus' (2:7). God is showing off. He wants the whole universe to see his grace (grace being God's kindness to us that we don't deserve).[15] We used to be 'by nature deserving of wrath', now we are trophies of grace, won by the death and resurrection of Jesus. Jesus took the wrath that we deserved upon himself, and rose to new life that we get to share in. Now, as all the powers in the heavenly realms look on, they will marvel at the character of God, and his rescue of us through grace.

---

15. I once heard someone describe the difference between mercy and grace this way: 'Mercy is not getting what we deserve. Grace is getting what we don't deserve.' With a passage that mentions both God's mercy and grace, I figured there was no better time to share that with you.

If that's not a satisfying turnaround to the most terrible predicament of all time, nothing will satisfy you!

SOMETHING TO REFLECT ON:
What does it mean to you that, because of God's mercy, you have been rescued from death and raised to be seated with Christ?

SOMETHING TO DO:
Spend some time praising God for his grace and mercy to you in Christ Jesus.

A PRAYER TO PRAY:
Merciful God, I praise you for your grace and kindness to me. May I never forget your rescue of me in your Son Jesus. Help me to reflect your glory to the world, as a living trophy of grace.

DAY ELEVEN

Famous

FOCUS VERSES: EPHESIANS 2:8–9

READ: Ephesians 2:1–10

SOME THINGS TO CONSIDER:
Have you ever seen a famous work of art in real life? I once went to a Van Gogh exhibition. I wasn't really into art, especially not painting, but I was into seeing famous stuff. My memories are of looking at *Starry Night* and *Sunflowers*, and thinking to myself, 'I'm seeing some of the world's most famous paintings in real life!' It felt pretty special, like I was now in some exclusive club of people who didn't just know about these paintings, or had merely seen them online or in a book, but had become part of their history, and they a part of mine.

When I get to verses like 8 and 9, I have a similar feeling. These are some of the most famous verses in the entire Bible. People sing about them, preach about them, memorise them, and argue about them. They have shaped the lives of Christians for thousands of years, and there they are, right there, in print, in the flesh. When I see them in the Bible, I get a zing of excitement that I get to read them. But what's more, I don't just get to read them – they apply to me. More than just looking at a famous piece of art, or reading a famous book, the truth of these verses affects me – it's like I have become part of the artwork or have discovered that I am a character in the book.

Why are these verses so famous? Read them again and see. Here is the promise that Paul is making: the way God has saved us from his wrath is 'by grace... through faith' (2:8). This is in contrast to works – you can't work for it, you can't earn it by doing lots of good things; grace is God's free gift to us and we get it only because God chooses to give it to us. You can't pray more, give more money away, stop swearing, or not have sex until you're married to earn the gift of being saved by God. The only way you receive it is through faith – that is, through trusting in what Jesus has done for us in his death and resurrection.

This is great news because having to earn salvation can only end in two ways. You may do a lot of good things, and then become proud and boastful because you think you're good enough to deserve God's love. Or you can fail at the good things you attempt to do and then fall into despair that you will never be good enough for God's love. Chances are, if you're anything like me, you swing between the two, some days feeling great about yourself, and superior to all the other sinners out there, other days feeling terrible about yourself, inferior to the 'good' Christians, and unloved by God. And whatever the case, you're never quite sure if you have done enough to earn God's salvation.

But being saved is a gift from God, so that no one can boast. This means you can't earn it, but you can be sure of it. You're saved, welcomed into God's family, forgiven for your sins, and part of God's eternal new creation, because when Jesus went to the cross he did everything necessary to make you right with God. All you have to do is put your faith in Jesus, trusting that his death and resurrection is enough (and even this faith is part of God's gift to you). He gives you what you need to trust in him. This is fantastic news!

Can you see now why these verses are so famous? And isn't it brilliant that they aren't just beautiful to look at like a great painting, or a magnificent sunrise, they are part of your story? God chose you before the world began to receive this gift. God has made you part of his story. Your salvation is part of God's extravagant artwork.

SOMETHING TO REFLECT ON:
In what ways does knowing that you do not have to earn God's salvation but that you receive it as a gift set you free? What does it set you free from?

Ephesians

SOMETHING TO DO:
There is nothing to do. Everything has been done for you by Jesus. Today, just enjoy yourself, knowing that you've been saved by God's free gift of grace.

A PRAYER TO PRAY:
Gracious God, thank you that we have been saved by your grace. Thank you that your salvation, and even the faith we have to receive it, is a free gift from you. Help me not to boast, but always rejoice in what you have done.

DAY TWELVE
Finding What You Were Made For

FOCUS VERSE: EPHESIANS 2:10

READ: Ephesians 2:1–10

SOME THINGS TO CONSIDER:
I went to the movies the other day and I was the only person in the cinema. This was very exciting!

But then, just minutes after my selfie, another man walked in. He sat down a row away from me. I was feeling a bit annoyed that my solo-cinema experience was being cramped. Throughout the whole film, he was on his phone, which annoyed me even more; just watch the movie, mate, that's why you're here. Then, right before the climax of the film, he got up and walked out! This man had zero respect for the cinema! How would he know what happened in the end? How would he know if the good guy won and saved the kid from the drug cartel gangsters? (He did by the way, phew!) I got the cinema to myself again, but I think I would have preferred that the man stayed and enjoyed the ending.

Often, people talk about, or memorise, Ephesians 2:8–9 but don't hang around for verse 10. This is like walking out before the end of the movie. Ephesians 2:10 is a vital verse in Paul's explanation of God's great reversal of our fortunes through the work of Jesus that he's been explaining since the beginning of chapter 2.

Yesterday we read: 'For it is by grace you have been saved, through faith – and this is not from yourselves, it is the gift of God – not by works, so that no one can boast' (2:8–9), which was fantastic news! Grace frees us from having to earn God's forgiveness and love. But that's not the end of the story.

'Hold on, hold on,' many people think when they hear the good news of verses 8–9. 'If I don't have to earn my salvation by being a good person, what even is the point of doing good things?'

It's a good question (I know because I wrote it). Notice what Paul says next: 'We are God's handiwork, created in Christ Jesus to do good works, which God prepared in advance for us to do' (2:10). We don't have to do good works to earn God's love, but we have been created by God to do good works. Getting saved comes first, but living the life you were created for comes next.

This is a pattern you can find throughout the Bible. Most famously, it was after God rescued his people from

Day Twelve: Finding What You Were Made For

slavery in the book of Exodus that he gave them the Ten Commandments. He didn't say, 'Obey me first, then I'll save you.' He saved them, so that they might then live for him. Now here in Ephesians we see the pattern repeated: being saved comes before being good.

What's more, these good works are not just something to keep you busy as you wait for heaven. No, we were created in Jesus to do them! First you get saved, then you live the life you were created for. This means if you want to feel really alive, you don't need to do something adrenaline-filled like jumping out of a plane or going to the movies by yourself, you only need to do the good works God has prepared for you to do. There is no better feeling than doing what God has created us to do.

What are these good works? Paul will explain in the second half of Ephesians. But for now, let's remember that all the things we may have done before to earn God's love – being kind and loving, caring for the poor, speaking out against injustice, praying for others, sharing the good news of Jesus – are transformed from things we feel *compelled* to do to things we *get to do* because we have been saved. These aren't just a random assortment of good things either. God has very specific good things that only we can do, which he has 'prepared in advance for us to do'. No one else can be the friend to your depressed mate that you can be. No group of friends can welcome the newly arrived refugee kid at school like you and your Christian mates can. No one can pray for the salvation of your family with the same heart you can.

This isn't to pressure you to make sure you discover what these good works are for fear of missing out on God's love. Think of it like an adventure, where you get to keep your eye out for the next instalment of God's plan of good works. Because it's what you were created for, you'll never feel more yourself than when you're doing the good works God prepared for you.

See how important Ephesians 2:10 is? We aren't just saved by grace (though we are); we are saved by grace to live for Jesus! So keep your eye out for what God has prepared for you to do. They are some of the best bits of being saved by Jesus.

SOMETHING TO REFLECT ON:
Looking back at your life as a Christian, what good works can you see that God prepared for you to do? How did you feel getting to do them?

SOMETHING TO DO:
Keep your eye out today for the good works that God has prepared for you to do. When you see them, do them! It's what you were made for.

A PRAYER TO PRAY:
Creator God, thank you that you did not save me just to sit around and wait for heaven, but I get to live in your new creation now as I do the good works you have prepared for me. Help me see them, do them, and experience the joy of doing what I was made for.

DAY THIRTEEN

Left Out

FOCUS VERSES: EPHESIANS 2:11-13

READ: Ephesians 2:11–22

SOME THINGS TO CONSIDER:
Have you ever been at home, with nothing to do, scrolling social media, when up pops one of your friend's stories? You see that all your mates are out having fun, but no one invited you. That hurts. Maybe they forgot to invite you. Perhaps they thought you had something else on. It could be, you worry, that they don't actually like you.

Paul, in today's passage, is trying to evoke that feeling of being left out. Not of missing out on hanging out with your friends, but an entire ethnic group of people missing out on every good thing God has on offer. That's a pretty big thing to miss out on.

In verses 11–13, Paul is speaking to his non-Jewish listeners, the Gentiles. While there were probably people in the Ephesian churches who were Jewish, many of them would not have been. The Gentiles wouldn't have grown up worshipping Yahweh (the Old Testament name for God) but pagan Greek and Roman gods. These people, Paul tells us, were known as the 'uncircumcised'. The Jews practiced circumcision on their male sons, which was a physical reminder of their religious and ethnic identity.[16] The Jews called the Gentiles the uncircumcised somewhat dismissively, because they weren't part of God's special promise to the people of Israel.[17]

Paul is reminding his readers how much they missed out on by not being part of God's people. He lists five things: not being with Christ (because Christ was a Jew); not being part of Israel (because they weren't Israelites); missing out on God's covenants (because God made his covenants with Israel); not having hope (because they were not part of the covenant); and not having God (because they did not know the true God). This is far worse than missing a trip to the beach or the movies with your mates. It's missing out on everything that God offers.

---

16. In case you're unsure, circumcision is where the foreskin that covers the head of the penis is cut off. Usually, it is performed in a religious ceremony when a boy is eight days old. My apologies if this footnote has made you feel a little awkward. At least I saved you googling it – that would be worse.

17. A covenant is a promise or agreement. In the Bible there are covenants made between God and his people. The covenants Paul is referring to here are the ones God made with the Ephesians' forefathers, Abraham, Isaac, Jacob, Israel, and David. They were promises that God would bless and never abandon them.

Day Thirteen: Left Out

You may feel like this is unfair. Like if all your friends were having a party, but you weren't invited just because you weren't the same race as them. You may even think that God's special deal with Israel was a little racist. But despite how it might seem, that's not how it was. Israel wasn't given a special relationship with God to hoard the blessings, but to be a light to all the nations (see Isaiah 49:6). They were to show the world the way to know God, so that through them all nations would receive God's blessings (see Genesis 12:2–3).

For a long time, this hadn't been happening very much. Sure, a few Gentiles became followers of Yahweh, but there was no mass influx of the uncircumcised into God's covenant promises. But what do we read in verse 13? 'But now in Christ Jesus you who once were far away have been brought near by the blood of Christ.' We may have been missing out before, but Jesus came to be the perfect embodiment of all the hopes and promises of the nation of Israel. Where Israel failed to be faithful to God, and to welcome Gentiles into God's family, Jesus, as the Jewish Messiah, made a way, through his death and resurrection, for all people, Jew or Gentile, to be saved. Finally, in Jesus, Israel was a light to the nations. In Jesus, all the nations of the world would be blessed. In Jesus, anyone can be brought near to God. No one has to miss out on any of the amazing blessings that are available. We can all be with Christ, citizens of God's nation, part of God's new covenant, with hope and with God. It turns out we have been invited to the salvation party after all!

Because of the work of Jesus, all of us, whatever our heritage, Jew and Gentile, can be part of God's chosen people. We all can be benefactors of the rich blessings of God. Despite how it may have once looked, no one has to miss out on all that God offers. You have not been left out.

SOMETHING TO REFLECT ON:
How would you feel if you could not receive God's blessings because you were not of the right ethnicity? How, then, do you feel knowing that Jesus' work means you, too, can be part of God's people?

SOMETHING TO DO:
Spend some time reflecting on your family heritage, and thank God, that through Jesus, you, and indeed anyone, can come near to God.

A PRAYER TO PRAY:
God of all nations, thank you that you always had a plan to include all people in your salvation promises. Thank you that Jesus has brought me into your family.

DAY FOURTEEN

The New Human

FOCUS VERSES: EPHESIANS 2:14–18

READ: Ephesians 2:11–22

SOME THINGS TO CONSIDER:
In year seven I had two friends who I would often hang out with. One was an Israeli Jew, and the other was a Pakistani Muslim. I didn't know a lot about politics, but I was aware that a Christian, a Jew, and a Muslim were not supposed to get along. I enjoyed walking around the school together feeling like we were a beacon of world peace, and I wondered why the politicians and the UN couldn't learn from us about how to get along.

Sadly, after a few years, both of them left the school, so we could no longer be a gang of religious harmony, but I hope if we hung out again we could all still be friends.

In today's passage, we read that Jesus is our peace. Not that Jesus brings peace, or Jesus makes peace, but 'he himself is our peace' (2:14). This is not just the peace you feel in yourself knowing that everything is right between you and God (though he does bring that peace), but a peace between people who do not always get on. Jesus is the worldwide solution to the problem I thought my friends and I were solving in high school.

Yesterday, we thought about how those of us who are not Jewish were previously excluded from God's blessings. The distinction between Jews and Gentiles was not just about religious differences, and the relationship often became hostile. The Jews would actively avoid and exclude Gentiles, and the Gentiles would often actively antagonise and persecute the Jews. But along came Jesus, and by his work on the cross, he destroyed any walls that might separate Jews and Gentiles.

In the Jewish Temple in Jerusalem, there was a wall separating the outermost court of the Temple from any of the more holy places. There were signs on the wall telling all Gentiles not to go past that point on penalty of death. That wall was itself a symbol of all the things in the Jewish law that excluded Gentiles from being part of God's family. When Jesus died at the cross, he fulfilled all the requirements of God's law that separate humans from God, but also that separate humans from each other. The people of God no longer need to be set apart and live differently by eating certain foods or only worshipping with the 'right' people. They can live in a way that embraces all people.

Day Fourteen: The New Human

The NIV translation of this passage says Jesus makes 'one new humanity' (2:15). However, in Greek, the original language, it says a 'new man'. Christians aren't just a new group of people, we are closer than that, we are as united as if we were one new person. We are not some kind of Frankenstein's monster, with all our different parts mashed together. Together, we are a whole, a brand-new person.

While Jesus has eliminated the hostility because Jew and Gentile, his work doesn't stop there. Because he makes a new humanity, he eliminated the hostility between all people. You may not spend a lot of time thinking about the differences between Jews and Gentiles, but I'm sure you've noticed hostility between different groups of people around you: people with differing political views, people of different races, people of different genders or views about gender, to name just a few. The good news is that Jesus unites all people who come to faith in him. There is no place for racism in the people of God, because Jesus has made us all one. There is also no place for sexism, ageism, ableism, or any other discriminatory -ism you can think of. Even people who like Pepsi are one with those of us who, correctly, prefer Coke.

This doesn't mean that Jesus eliminates all differences. A Sudanese Christian is still Sudanese. A German Christian is still German. I'm still a white, Australian man, but first and foremost, I am a Christian. My identity as a new creation in Jesus gives me more in common with a Latina, single mother in Ecuador who loves Jesus, or a Christian Chinese businessman in Beijing, than it does with the white guy who lives in the apartment across the hall from me (and that's not just because I'm not a huge fan of his taste in music).[18]

In Jesus, we can celebrate our differences. A Sudanese, German, Latin American, and Chinese Christian will each have unique experiences and insights into the person of Jesus that I can learn from. We no longer need to be threatened by people who are different. What we have in common is greater, on a cosmic level, than what makes us different, so we all get to benefit from each other's love of Jesus.

Of course, that doesn't mean it's all easy going. We all bring cultural baggage to our new humanity, which will sometimes make our relationships tense. But because Jesus has united us all to God and to each other, we get to learn to live out our interpersonal peace, together.

SOMETHING TO REFLECT ON:
Where have you seen this new humanity, with people of different races, genders, ages, abilities, and many other kinds of backgrounds coming together because of Jesus? Does your church reflect this new humanity?

SOMETHING TO DO:
Consider and act on what you can do to build relationships with Christians who are different from you, so that together you might enjoy the unity that Jesus brings us.

---

[18]. Of course, he could be a Christian, in which case, we do have a lot in common. This shows how bad a neighbour I am. I haven't got to know him enough to know if he's a Christian, only enough to know that I don't like his taste in music.

A PRAYER TO PRAY:

God of all humanity, thank you that Jesus is our peace. Forgive me for the times I have caused division among your people. Help me to live in a way that reflects your love for all people and the new humanity that Jesus has created in all of us who love and follow you.

DAY FIFTEEN

Feels Like Home

FOCUS VERSES: EPHESIANS 2:19–22

READ: Ephesians 2:11–22

SOME THINGS TO CONSIDER:
Two days ago, we thought about what it feels like to be left out. Today we're thinking about a much better feeling, the feeling of belonging. In high school, I never much felt like I belonged. However, every now and again, something would happen that made me feel like it was my place. Once, a girl I knew from church came to my school to play sport – her school versus my school. Seeing as she was at my school, I showed her around like I owned the place. I said 'Hi' to everyone that we walked past, even the people I only vaguely knew. I wanted her to be impressed with how popular and at ease I was at my school.

Most of the time, when we feel like we belong, it doesn't require showing off. You don't have to think about it or pretend at all. It's part of your identity, like being in a loving family, or a part of a caring group of friends. You're in, you're home, you're safe.

Because Jesus has made us one humanity with all other Christians, and because he has given us access to our heavenly Father, we all belong to the community of God. In today's passage, Paul gives his readers three metaphors for what it means to belong to the people of God, each one of increasing intimacy.

The first is that of being citizens of God's nation. You may have experienced the excitement of going overseas. Being in a foreign country is fun, but it can be stressful. When you don't know the language or the customs, the new culture can be exciting, but you do not feel like you belong. You feel like a foreigner and a stranger, because that's what you are. That is what we were in relation to the people of God. But now, because of Jesus, we have become citizens. When you return to your country from overseas, as you hear people speaking in your language with your accent, you know you're home. You feel safe; you feel like you're back where you belong. That's what Jesus has done for us. He's made us citizens of God's nation.

However, despite feeling at home in your own country, it's nothing compared to Paul's second metaphor, the feeling of belonging you get with your own family. These are the people who know all your quirks and put up with your music choices. They've smelt your morning breath, experienced your bad moods, and they still love you. In Jesus, we are part of God's household. When you're in Jesus, you're home.

The last image is the one of the most intimacy. Paul, who doesn't seem to care about mixing metaphors at all, says that we aren't just members of a household, we are bricks in God's house, and Jesus is the chief brick. He's the cornerstone. This was the foundational stone by which every angle and wall in the building is aligned.

Now, you may think being a brick doesn't seem more intimate than being part of a family. But consider how close to each other bricks in a building are. They're all stacked on top of each other, bearing each other's loads. Each one plays an important role in completing the building. And what is that building in Paul's metaphor? It's the temple of God. It's where God dwells. God doesn't live on some faraway cloud, or in some fabulous church in a foreign country. God has chosen to live in us by his Holy Spirit. That means, if you have put your trust in Jesus, God is never far away because he lives among us.

Can you see what I mean by belonging? As Christians, we aren't just alone in the world trying to find somewhere to belong. We have a God who has saved us, we are citizens of a heavenly nation, we're members of an eternal family, and we're part of the temple of God in which he lives. You can't belong anywhere better than that.

SOMETHING TO REFLECT ON:
How does knowing about the depth of your belonging change how you see yourself, your fellow Christians, and God?

SOMETHING TO DO:
Not every Christian feels like they belong, despite the spiritual reality we've read about today. What is one thing you can do today to help someone else feel a sense of belonging among God's people?

A PRAYER TO PRAY:
Father God, thank you that I belong to you along with every other Christian. Thank you that Jesus was willing to be rejected, and to become an outsider, so that I might belong to your people. Help me have a deep sense of my belonging, so that I might help others feel at home among your people.

DAY SIXTEEN

Mystery Solved

FOCUS VERSES: EPHESIANS 3:1-6

READ: Ephesians 3:1–13

SOME THINGS TO CONSIDER:
I once heard a story about a man who, when he had a shower, seemingly from nowhere, coins would fall to the floor between his feet. It was like they just fell straight out of the shower head. As he collected his small jackpot of coins, he would wonder how he had been lucky enough to get a magic shower.

This mystery enthralled and perplexed me. I was also excited that perhaps I could get myself a cash shower and make a lot of money. However, as the story progressed, the mystery was revealed. At night, the guy would fall asleep with his pants on and his shirt off. All the spare change in his pocket would fall out and get stuck to his back as he slept. Then in the shower, the coins fell off. He wasn't finding new money, he was just finding his old money again. It was disappointing that his shower wasn't magic, but at least the mystery was solved.[19]

The story of the cash shower is a good little mystery, with a satisfying conclusion. You may have noticed that in today's passage, Paul uses the word mystery three times. The mystery he is talking about, however, is no minor mystery, like the coin guy. Nor is it even a large mystery like a true crime podcast about some unsolved murder. It's the biggest of all mysteries. But one that has now been solved because God has revealed it to him.

In the time before Jesus' arrival, Israel's prophets made it clear that God was going to save his people. They also hinted at the fact that God would save all people, whether or not they were an Israelite. The mystery was: how? How was God going to achieve such a momentous outcome? Paul is claiming to have had the answer revealed to him – and the other apostles and prophets[20] – by the Holy Spirit.

What is the solution to this mystery? It's Jesus! Because of the work of Jesus in his death and resurrection, all people can be full members of God's people. You may

---

19. You can listen to the story yourself if you want: 'No Coincidence, No Story!', *This American Life*, 489, 1 March 2013. https://www.thisamericanlife.org/489/no-coincidence-no-story/act-three-14

20. These prophets are not the Old Testament prophets, like Isaiah and Jeremiah, but the New Testament prophets, the ones who were given the gift of prophecy (1 Corinthians 12:10, 28–29). These were people through whom the Holy Spirit spoke, affirming Jesus' role in uniting Jews and Gentiles.

Day Sixteen: Mystery Solved

think, 'I know, we already covered this yesterday and the day before.' But hopefully you'll forgive Paul for getting excited about this. I heard about the shower coin mystery almost a decade ago, and I still think about it; the problem of Gentiles being excluded from God's people had been an issue for thousands of years.

Before Paul had 'the mystery made known to [him] by revelation' (3:3) he was a devout Jew. He was so committed to his faith that he was killing Christians because he was sure they were perverting the true religion. Paul thought anyone who wasn't a Jew was unclean and destined for destruction. But then the resurrected Jesus confronted him on the road to Damascus (see Acts 9:1–19) and revealed the mystery to Paul that all people can come to salvation in him, and can share in all the same blessings as Israel. Ever since, Paul had devoted his life to helping Gentiles put their faith in Jesus. So much so that as he wrote Ephesians, he was a prisoner because of this commitment. Paul was locked up and was awaiting trial before Caesar because he had been (falsely) accused of taking a Gentile into the Jewish Temple. (It's a long story that you can read about in Acts, starting in chapter 21.)

Paul was willing to suffer because he was convinced that this mystery was world-changing stuff. And indeed it was. Most people in the world today who know Jesus would have been excluded had not this mystery been revealed. The world is a different place now because God has made a way for all of us to be 'sharers together in the promise in Christ Jesus' (3:6). That's a treasure that's even better than coins magically appearing in the shower, with an infinitely more satisfying conclusion. How wonderful that God and his people have done what is necessary so that we would know this mystery!

SOMETHING TO REFLECT ON:
Paul was willing to lose his freedom, and ultimately his life, to share the mystery of Jesus with Gentiles. What sacrifices have you made to help others know the good news of Jesus?

SOMETHING TO DO:
Think of one thing you can do to help others discover the good news that all people are welcome in God's family. Perhaps it's inviting a friend to youth group or church, or offering to read the Bible with a family member. Do one thing today to help someone else discover the mystery.

A PRAYER TO PRAY:
God of Revelation, thank you that you have revealed your wonderful plan to welcome anyone into your family through Jesus. Help me to never lose the excitement of being saved by Jesus. Help my excitement overflow into helping other people meet Jesus too, even if it costs me, just as it did for Paul.

DAY SEVENTEEN
The Universe is Watching

FOCUS VERSES: EPHESIANS 3:7–13

READ: Ephesians 3:1–13

SOME THINGS TO CONSIDER:
At school, I wasn't particularly popular, and I felt like most of my classmates didn't know the 'real me'. While there were the kids who were cool, good looking, and got to date each other, I was a fringe dweller. I had plans of becoming a big shot Hollywood director, so I would imagine turning up to my ten-year high school reunion having achieved brilliant success in the film industry. All those people who had underestimated me in school would see the manifold wisdom of my life plan. They would realise that all those hours I spent making short

films were, in fact, just the first steps in my billion-dollar career.

Unfortunately for my movie business career, God had other plans, and I never became an Academy Award-winning director. But fortunately for me, my class has never had a reunion.[21] If I were to meet all my classmates today, I'd have to admit that I never lived out my film-making dreams (if anyone actually remembered that I had them) and my greatest claim to fame is that I'm a very low-selling author of Bible books who once was in the background of his cousin's viral video.

Of course, God's plans are better than my plans, and I'm sure I'm much happier doing what I do than whatever I had planned for myself. God's plans have a way of being much more impressive than anything we could ever dream.

Paul writes in today's passage about a much more dramatic life direction change than mine. Paul went from being a guy who killed Christians to someone who preached Christ, even to the point of death. He did it so that Gentiles, like Jews, would come to know of Jesus and how they could be saved. They could get, as Paul teaches, the 'boundless riches of Christ' (3:8). That's pretty darn good.

Paul has spent a lot of time telling us about all the great things we get when we are in Christ: forgiveness, membership in God's family, the Holy Spirit living in us. And now we find out we have boundless riches, riches that are uncountable, there is no end to them. Imagine turning up to your school reunion and telling your class you are

---

21. At least, they haven't had a reunion that I know of. There is a chance there have been reunions and no one invited me.

so rich you can't begin to assess how rich you are. That's how rich we are in Jesus. Not only that, we get unfettered, confident access to God in Jesus (3:12). That's even better than having the ear of the Prime Minister or President. Riches and power, except without the corruption earthly riches and power bring? Could you hope for more?

Well, there is more! We're told that the Church has a role. It's not just doing the work of Jesus here on earth, but a role in the heavenly realms. It's the job of the Church to show all the spiritual powers, both good and bad, the wisdom of God. Just as Jesus' death and resurrection made a spectacle of all the evil powers that stood against the work of God (see Colossians 2:13–15), when people of all races, even the people groups who have the greatest enmity, gather united in Jesus, all the spiritual powers can see the magnificence of what God accomplished in Jesus. It's like God showing up to the reunion of all the powers of the universe – the angels, the demons, and even Satan – and showing us off as his magnificent accomplishment. Satan and his demons like to drive wedges between ethnic, political, or age groups, and between individuals. Jesus undoes all the work of Satan as he makes peace between everyone. Even the most hateful divisions are healed in the spiritual realm, and with the Spirit's help, we can live out that healing here on earth.

Finally, Paul asks his readers not to be discouraged, because his sufferings are for their glory. Paul was willing to suffer in prison, to preach Christ to his peril, because he knew that all the glory he has described in the letter so far is on offer for those who would believe his message about Jesus. What might look like defeat now, in God's power, is for the sake of glory. In the earthly realm, the life of a Christian may not look all that amazing, but in the heavenly realm, where reality can be clearly seen, God's wisdom is shown off in the life of God's people. Whatever dreams of life success you may have to impress your high school friends, remember that in Jesus, you're a trophy, showing off the wisdom and goodness of God. In Jesus, you've done alright.

SOMETHING TO REFLECT ON:
The unity of the Church is a display of God's wisdom to the watching heavenly powers. If people on earth are watching you and your relationships with other Christians, would they be able to see God's wisdom on display in the way you love each other?

SOMETHING TO DO:
Ask God to make clear how you can live out his unity among his people. When he lets you know, make sure you get to it today.

A PRAYER TO PRAY:
God of wisdom, help me and my fellow Christians live in a way that makes your wisdom known to those who are watching in the heavenly realms and here on earth. Show me how I can live out our unity among your people.

DAY EIGHTEEN

There's Always More

FOCUS VERSES: EPHESIANS 3:14–19

READ: Ephesians 3:14–21

SOME THINGS TO CONSIDER:
Scientists tell us that the universe is constantly expanding. One astronomer, Dr Wendy Freedman, calculated that the universe is expanding at a rate of '72 kilometres per second per megaparsec'.[22] As I have no way of measuring that myself, I'll take her word for it. I don't understand exactly what it means, but as far as I can tell, if I got in a starship and left earth today, plotting a course for the edge of the universe, when I made it there the edge wouldn't

---

22. Dennis Overbye, 'Cosmos Controversy: The Universe is Expanding, But How Fast?', *The New York Times,* 20 February 2017. https://www.nytimes.com/2017/02/20/science/hubble-constant-universe-expanding-speed.html

be there anymore. It would have moved on. Even if I did manage to reach the edge of the universe, it wouldn't be the edge for long. There would always be more universe.

At the beginning of chapter 3, Paul started praying but got side-tracked talking about how God has saved the Gentiles. Now, he's back on task. As he prays, he's asking for the spiritual equivalent of reaching the edge of the universe. Paul is praying for the Ephesian churches to fully know God, that they might catch the uncatchable and fathom the unfathomable. It's an impossible task. Whenever you think you've got a grasp on God, you look up and the horizon has moved. There's always more. More love, more wisdom, more power. More, more, more. But despite the impossibility of his request, Paul's not afraid to ask.

Paul begins by saying that he kneels before the Father (3:14). We don't just pray with our minds and our voices, our whole bodies are part of the process, and Paul takes a posture of humility before God. The Bible shows us people praying in all sorts of positions – standing, kneeling, lying down – so it may be worth thinking about your posture when you pray. Maybe try kneeling next time – see how it changes your prayer time.

Paul prays that the Ephesian churches might be strengthened 'so that Christ may dwell in your hearts through faith' (3:17). But if they're already Christians, doesn't Jesus already live in them by the Holy Spirit? It's true that when we become Christian, Jesus dwells in us, but what's probably going on here is like the difference between staying at someone's house as a guest and living

Day Eighteen: There's Always More

in your own home. Guests have somewhere to sleep but they don't get to run the place. We can allow Jesus to live in us, but we need Jesus to move in. He has to renovate our lives – to replace the broken windows, put in a new kitchen, and replace your ghastly wallpaper. Jesus wants to take over every part of our lives that we haven't yet handed over to him.

How will he do that? By giving us the power to fully comprehend his love. The better we understand his love, the more of our lives we'll be likely to hand over to him. What does it mean to know the width, length, height, and depth of this love? The late, great John Stott put it like this:

> It seems to me legitimate to say that the love of Christ is 'broad' enough to encompass all mankind (especially Jews and Gentiles, the theme of these chapters), 'long' enough to last for eternity, 'deep' enough to reach the most degraded sinner, and 'high' enough to exult him to heaven.[23]

But as good as Uncle Stott's quote is, it still doesn't do justice to the love of Christ. That's because this love 'surpasses knowledge' (3:19). No matter how much of Jesus' love you know, you'll never reach its edge. There is always more. Paul is asking for the impossible. In fact, Paul finishes the paragraph with another impossible

---

23. John Stott, *The Message of Ephesians* (Nottingham: Inter-Varsity Press, 1979), 137.

request – that the Ephesian Christians 'may be filled to the measure of all the fullness of God' (3:19). How can you be filled with the fullness of an eternal God? You can't, it's too great, it's too much. We will never know all God's power, we will never understand all his love, and we will never be filled with all his fullness. But that doesn't mean we can't ask for it. We have an eternity with God ahead of us, in this life and the next. We have an eternity to discover his glorious riches and be filled with his fullness. Time to get in your starship.

SOMETHING TO REFLECT ON:
What parts of your life are you struggling to hand over to Jesus? How would a better understanding of his love and power help you allow him to be at home in all of your life?

SOMETHING TO DO:
Take some time to pray today's passage for one or two people in your life, that they might know more of God's power, understand Jesus' love, and be filled with all the fullness of God. This might be a prayer you'd like to memorise and pray regularly.

A PRAYER TO PRAY:
Eternal God, thank you that you have made yourself knowable. Help me know more of you every day – more of your love and power. Fill me up with your fullness so that you might be at home in all my life.

DAY NINETEEN

The End of Part One

FOCUS VERSES: EPHESIANS 3:20–21

READ: Ephesians 3:14–21

SOME THINGS TO CONSIDER:
I went to a play recently which was actually two plays.[24] It had a part one and part two and they made you buy tickets to both performances if you wanted to see the entire story. Usually plays will just have an intermission, but this one had a three-hour break, and cost twice as much money. I think maybe the producers were merely trying to double their dollars.

Part one ended with a cliffhanger. The main characters had made a vital discovery which would

---

24. The plays were *Harry Potter and the Cursed Child: Parts 1 and 2* in case you're interested.

change the dynamic of the story from then on. It was very dramatic (which I guess is appropriate when you're watching dramatic theatre) and I couldn't wait to get back to the theatre for part two, even if the two parts were just a ploy to get more money out of suckers like me.

At this point in Ephesians, we have reached a turning point. This is the end of part one. If there was a time to go out to the lobby and get yourself a tiny Coke and some over-priced chips, this is it. Paul has spent the last three chapters telling us about all the amazing things God has done for us, and what it means for our identity and unity as his people. These amazing revelations are going to change the dynamic of everything he says from now on, and hopefully, the dynamic of our lives, too. If chapters 1–3 of Ephesians are the theory of what it means to be 'in Christ', chapters 4–6 are the practical outworking of that theory.

Paul ends this half of the letter, appropriately, in praise. To change metaphors, this is the high point of the letter. We've reached the summit, after this we're heading down the mountain, back to ground level. On the way, we're going to learn how to live our lives in response. But what is at the peak? It's praise for God, who is able to do 'immeasurably more than all we ask or imagine' (3:20).

I hate asking people for things. I always worry that I'll offend them by asking too much, or just by making a request at all. Whether or not my awkwardness with other humans is valid, it's got no place with God. You can never ask for too much with God. In fact, the biggest thing you could even think of asking for, God can do

Day Nineteen: The End of Part One

even more. Try it. Imagine the biggest thing you can think of. God can do it. That doesn't mean he will, but he would if he thought it was good for you.

But you know what is even more than we could ever have asked for or imagined that God would do? that he would save us by his eternal Son becoming human himself. Jesus Christ gave his life to save us, and bring us into his family, and to make us a part of him! Can you imagine asking the Father, 'Hey God, would you mind sending your Son to die for me even though I deserve death? And while you're at it, can he rise to new life so that I might also rise like him? Oh and one more thing: can I be included "in him" so that I might reign with him in the heavenly realms? Thanks!' What an absurd thing to ask for! We would never have imagined it was possible if God hadn't already done it for us.

Now the same power that saved us, and raised Jesus from the dead (1:19–20), is in us! How can we not be moved to praise God? And how can we not also be assured that whatever life he is calling us to in the following chapters is entirely within our reach, because God's power is at work in us? God's future for us is bright!

SOMETHING TO REFLECT ON:
What has been the most life-changing truth you have learnt in the first half of Ephesians? How have you seen it changing how you see God, yourself, and others?

Ephesians

SOMETHING TO DO:
Look back through Ephesians 1–3. Choose one verse to memorise which will encourage you as you seek to live for Jesus, especially as you take seriously the call to new living in Ephesians 4–6.

A PRAYER TO PRAY:
Now, to you Lord, who is able to do immeasurably more than all we ask or imagine, according to your power that is at work within us, to you be glory in the church and in Christ Jesus throughout all generations, for ever and ever! Amen.

DAY TWENTY

Unified With Them?

FOCUS VERSES: EPHESIANS 4:1–6

READ: Ephesians 4:1–16

SOME THINGS TO CONSIDER:
What's your calling? Is it to be a famous YouTuber? A powerful CEO? A great parent? A competitive eater? A world-class worship leader? If you feel called to greatness, excellent. Read on. God has called you to greatness, but it may not be exactly the greatness you're hoping for.

As we begin the second half of Ephesians, Paul calls on the Ephesian Christians to live a life 'worthy of the calling they have received' (4:1). All the stuff he's just told them in the previous three chapters about what God has done for them, all the blessings they have in Jesus, and how Jews and Gentiles have been brought together, is not just interesting trivia, it is their calling. They have been called to be children of God and co-heirs with Christ. They have been called to one new humanity where all people of all races are one in Jesus.

So what does it mean to live out this calling? Paul calls on his readers to 'Make every effort to keep the unity of the Spirit through the bond of peace' (4:3). We are all unified together, as one new humanity, through the Holy Spirit. But now we must live out that unity in the way we treat each other. Unity is not just theory, it's practical. As Christians, we are not one new humanity in some nice, feel-good, abstract sense of being one with all Christians everywhere (though that is true). We are one with the annoying person at church who talks too much. And we're one with the Christians at the church down the road that you don't like. We're also one with the old person in your church who has political views that make you angry, and the person at youth group hasn't quite figured out how deodorant works yet.

How do we live this unity out? In verse 2, Paul gives us three key attitudes which will allow us to keep unity: 1) Humility, because when each of us puts others before ourselves, we'll have an entire community that looks after each other, not just themselves; 2) Gentleness – which is strength under control – because all of us have power and we must use it for the good of others. We must be helpers, not abusers; 3) Patience, because there will be tensions in every group of Christians (especially in the case of the ancient church where there were the deep-grained ethnic tensions between Jews and Gentiles) and we need to hold our tongue and our temper, choosing to love even the most testing of our brothers and sisters.

In verses 4–6, Paul explains why we must maintain unity. It's not just because life goes better when everyone is humble, gentle, and patient (though it does), but because our oneness reflects the oneness of God (who is three persons in one God – Father, Son, Holy Spirit), and the oneness of our faith. We are one body, the body of Christ, because all Christians, through the one Spirit living in them, are united to each other. We have one hope, because all of us will be resurrected like the risen King Jesus. We have one Lord in Jesus, who has united us to one faith. There is not one Christianity for the Jews and one for Gentiles, nor one for the conservatives and one for the liberals, or one for the weird Holy Spirit people and one for the people who love the Bible. There is only the Lord Jesus, whom we put our trust in, and in whose death and new life we are baptised. Everything expresses that one faith. Finally, giving life and power to all we do and all there is, is God the Father, our one true Father in heaven. These are the things which bring us all together in unity.

The unity of God's people is rarely found in big, inspiring acts of solidarity like, for instance, Christians all around the world making virtual choirs in the middle of a global pandemic,[25] but in the small, everyday acts of love that we show towards each other. We 'keep the unity of the Spirit' (4:3) among the Christians we know and go to church with by forgiving the people who have hurt

---

[25]. If you have no idea what I'm talking about, search YouTube for 'The Blessing Virtual Choir' and you'll see what I mean.

us, and asking forgiveness of those we have hurt. Unity is expressed by mending broken relationships, and being patient and kind to those who annoy us the most. We are all one in Jesus. Our challenge is to live a life worthy of our calling.

SOMETHING TO REFLECT ON:
How does this passage challenge your view of your calling? How are you living a life worthy of your calling in Jesus?

SOMETHING TO DO:
We're called to be unified. Reflecting on the questions above, choose something practical you can do to 'keep the unity of the Spirit' with your fellow Christians, and do it in the next week.

A PRAYER TO PRAY:
God, Father, Son, and Holy Spirit, thank you that in your unity you show us how we might love one another. Help me live a life worthy of my calling by loving my sisters and brothers in Christ with humility, gentleness, and patience.

DAY TWENTY-ONE

Socks and a Magic Axe

FOCUS VERSES: EPHESIANS 4:7-13

READ: Ephesians 4:1–16

SOME THINGS TO CONSIDER:
My dad (Pop) used to go on a lot of work trips. He would fly around the world and do stuff in loads of different countries. He was an engineer, and not knowing exactly what he did, I imagined him visiting worksites, wearing a hardhat, looking at plans, and pointing at stuff. When he came home from these trips, he always brought a gift for each of his kids. As he walked in the door, I would run up to him, pretending to be excited to see him, but really just hoping he would give me my present.

In today's passage, we read about Jesus returning from the most impressive trip ever. Not from one country to another, but from heaven to earth and back again.

In verse 8, Paul quotes from Psalm 68, where God is portrayed as a victorious military leader. Here, Jesus is that conquering hero, having defeated the powers of evil and death during his time on earth. And then he returns home, ascending to heaven, giving gifts to his people – the spoils of victory.

I can't remember what my dad brought me from his travels, but these days he and my mum bring me socks if they go on a trip. What gifts does Jesus give? They are 'the apostles, the prophets, the evangelists, the pastors and teachers' (4:11). These are people gifted by Jesus to the Church, to equip us to live out his calling. It's like the Church is a band of adventurers sent on a quest and Jesus hands over some gifts, saying, 'You'll need these for the journey!' Except we aren't given magic axes or invisibility cloaks, we're given people (who are probably more helpful than magical artefacts in the long run).

Who are these people? First, we have apostles. Apostle means 'sent one'. When we talk about the apostles (the eleven disciples, Mathias – Judas' replacement – and Paul), they are people sent by God to be witnesses to the resurrected Jesus and establish new churches. We might not have with us today the original apostles who met the resurrected Jesus in the flesh, but we do have people who establish new churches and new ministries within God's Kingdom. They may not be called apostles, but they still do important work. As the world keeps growing and changing, we need these people to help us start new churches and ministries. They help the Church grow and evolve.

Day Twenty-one: Socks and a Magic Axe

Next, we have prophets. These are people whose gift is helping the Church hear and understand what God wants to say to his people and the world right now. While there were the prophets in the Old Testament, God still has things to say to us today, and he uses those with the gift of prophesy. We need prophets to call us to faithfulness and help us understand what God is doing in the world.

Then we have the evangelists. These are people gifted in sharing the good news of what Jesus has done. While all Christians are to be witnesses to the work of Christ, some people have a particular calling and are especially gifted to help people know and understand what Jesus has done. We need people like this to help us all obey Jesus' command to bring his good news to the world (see Acts 1:8).

Lastly, we have the pastors and teachers. These two go together. A pastor cares for a church, like a shepherd cares for their sheep, leading and guiding them. Just as a flock of sheep requires a shepherd to make sure they stick together safely and have food and protection, pastors are needed to play this role spiritually in the lives of Christians. One way to do this is through teaching God's people who he is and how to follow him, hence the need for teachers. In the Bible, people called to lead churches are always required to be able to teach God's truth to others (see 1 Timothy 3:1–7; Titus 1:6–9), but not all people who are able to teach are called to lead churches. There are teachers who aren't pastors, but there shouldn't be pastors who aren't teachers.

These five types of people are Jesus' gift to every Christian to equip us to do the work Jesus gave us in order that we will be unified together (which is a big job seeing as Christians are often fighting with each other). Our unity comes not only by being kind to each other but by recognising that we all worship Jesus and we're all seeking to know him more (4:13). When Jesus returns, we will be unified and know Jesus fully, as completely mature Christians. Until then, as we grow, we can be thankful that we have people who are equipping us along the way. They are Jesus' gift to us – a whole lot better than socks, and at least ten per cent better than a magic axe. Thanks, Jesus!

SOMETHING TO REFLECT ON:
Who are the apostles, prophets, evangelists, and pastors and teachers who have helped you and your church do the work of Jesus? Could Jesus be calling you to one of these roles?

SOMETHING TO DO:
Spend some time thanking God for the people he has put in your life, to equip you and other Christians to serve Jesus. If you think you might be called to one of these roles, talk to someone older and wiser, like your pastor or youth leader, and ask them to help you figure out your next steps.

Day Twenty-one: Socks and a Magic Axe

A PRAYER TO PRAY:

God in heaven, thank you that Jesus has given us everything we need to live out your mission as your people from the bounty of his victory against the powers of the evil. Thank you for the apostles, prophets, evangelists, and pastors and teachers who have helped me know Jesus better. If you are calling me to one of these roles, please make it clear to me, and help me obey your call.

DAY TWENTY-TWO

Are You Grown Up?

FOCUS VERSES: EPHESIANS 4:14–16

READ: Ephesians 4:1–16

SOME THINGS TO CONSIDER:
How do you know when you're mature? Maybe maturity is being able to change a car tyre, or have a disagreement with your mum without yelling or crying, or enjoying reading about politics. I remember the first time I could drive by myself, I felt very mature. I drove home, picked up my baby sister (who my mum had asked me to mind), then headed to my friend's house. My sister was not fully toilet trained yet, and she wee-ed on the car seat. So I arrived at my friend's, cleaned up the wee, then drove home. It wasn't the hooning freedom I was excited about, but it was better than driving my parents around while I learnt to drive.

In this passage, Paul explains what Christian maturity looks like. First, he tells us what it's not. It's not being 'tossed back and forth by the waves, and blown here and there by every wind of teaching and by the cunning and craftiness of people in their deceitful scheming' (4:14).

There are many people saying dodgy stuff out there. Like Christian patriotism that says your love for Jesus is bound up in how well you love your country. Or universalism, which teaches that it doesn't matter whether or not you trust in Jesus, you will be saved anyway. Or false teachers who ask you for money so they can bless you or give you the secrets of the faith. You only have to hang out on YouTube for a bit, or follow a few angry hashtags, to find yourself heading down some sub-Christian rabbit hole. These may seem like new phenomena, but as you can see from verse 14, people who misuse the Christian faith to gain power, influence, or money from immature Christians have been around since the beginning of our faith.

So how do we avoid this? We become mature. Maturity comes from 'speaking the truth in love' (4:15). If an immature person attempts to speak the truth to themselves, they will only encourage themselves in their own immaturity. Just like if you got a year one class to write their own textbooks, things would not go well. But thankfully we can always find someone more mature than us. There have been women and men listening to Jesus, studying the Bible, and learning what it means to follow him for thousands of years. The apostles,

Day Twenty-two: Are You Grown Up?

prophets, evangelists, and pastors and teachers have been given to us to help us mature. The whole body of Jesus, that is, all Christians, have an obligation to speak the truth of Jesus from God's word, with love. And the whole body of Jesus has an obligation to listen to that truth. As we hear the truth of Jesus, told to us with love, not from someone's selfish desire for power, influence, or money, we will grow into maturity. Having heard the truth of Jesus, we now have an obligation to pass it on, in love, to others. As this cycle continually happens, together every Christian grows as the one body of Jesus.

We can see the best example of what 'truth in love' looks like in the life of Jesus. He spoke truth with total love. He didn't exploit people for his own gain, but instead, his commitment to truth and love cost him his life.

So how do you know if someone is speaking the truth in love? Here are three simple questions to ask:

> 1. Is it truthful? (Does it line up with what is in the Bible?)
> 2. Is it loving? (Does it cost the speaker for the benefit of the hearer, or does it attempt to take from the hearer for the benefit of the speaker?)
> 3. Does it glorify Jesus? (Is the speaker seeking to help you know, love, and follow Jesus, or something or someone else?)

Being a mature Christian is not some unattainable goal for only old people who have spent their whole life reading their Bible and praying. Jesus wants all of us to grow together to be his mature body. If you're careful to watch out for people who will take advantage of you, and you're committed to listening to and being changed by the loving truth of Jesus, you will grow to be the mature Christian God is calling you to be.

SOMETHING TO REFLECT ON:
What deceptive or exploitative false teaching have you encountered? What kind of deceptive and exploitative teaching would you be most likely to listen to?

SOMETHING TO DO:
Consider who are the trustworthy, mature Christians you know personally. Ask if you can meet up with one of them to hear how they grow in maturity. Who knows, they could even become a mentor to you, helping you grow in your faith.

A PRAYER TO PRAY:
God of all truth, help me grow in maturity as I take my place in Jesus' body. Help me not to be fooled by lies, but listen to the truth in love, so that I can pass that truth on, and help others to grow in maturity too.

DAY TWENTY-THREE

Living the Dream

FOCUS VERSES: EPHESIANS 4:17–24

READ: Ephesians 4:17–5:2

SOME THINGS TO CONSIDER:
For years, I had a recurring dream. I would dream that I was back at school, and my teachers were making me go to class, do tests, and were bossing me around. I would have a terrible time until I remembered I don't go to school anymore, and I could leave whenever I wanted. So I'd stand up, yell at the teacher, and sometimes cry or kick them in the shins. Then I would run out of the school a free man. It was always very cathartic.

    I haven't had the school dream in a while, but I do have similar dreams about fleeing old workplaces that I didn't like. I can tell you, throwing off your past is a very satisfying feeling.

In today's passage, Paul tells the Ephesians they need to leave their old life. As people who were dead in their sins (2:1), given new life by Jesus (2:5), and seated with him in the heavenly realms (2:6), they now had a new way to live. This new way of life is not just a suggestion from Paul, but a command of Jesus (4:17).

Paul reminds them of what the life of someone who is not in relationship with God looks like. It's a life characterised by ignorance and separation from God, because they have a heart that refuses to worship him. This leads people to a spiritual numbness. When Paul wrote verse 19 in the original Greek, he used a word that means calloused. Like when a callous builds up on your skin – you can prick it with a needle and feel no pain. Because people live in rebellion against God, they lose the ability to feel him calling them to choose right over wrong. As a result, they will do terrible things. They'll indulge all their selfish desires and call it love, they'll take more than they deserve and claim it as their right, they'll ignore the needs of others and call it living responsibly. It's a downward spiral, from being made in God's image, to living a life of evil and naming it the good life.[26]

Is Paul saying that everything a non-Christian does is evil? No! If you look around the world you can see plenty of evil, but you can also see plenty of good, because everyone

---

[26]. For a more in-depth look at this spiral of depravity, you can read Romans 1:18–32 where Paul goes into more detail. It's not really cheery reading though.

Day Twenty-three: Living the Dream

has the image of God within them. Paul isn't saying that all people live a life as bad as the one he describes all the time, just that all rebellion against God will lead us further down the spiral. The natural end point for a life of ignoring God is not becoming a good person apart from God, but a life of total selfishness lived caring nothing for the pain your choices cause in the world.

So is Paul saying that everything a Christian does is good? No, again! Sometimes we Christians do terrible things. You only need to look at the history of the Church to see that. When we do the wrong thing, we're still living in our old way of life and giving in to our 'deceitful desires' (4:22). Until Jesus returns to fully transform us to be like him, the remnants of our old life will still be in us. That's the whole reason Paul is writing these paragraphs; because we're not perfect people. He's reminding us we can't live our old life anymore.

So what are we to do? Since we became Christians, hopefully we've had people teaching us about who Jesus is, and how to follow him. When you become a Christian, it's not like buying a Scottish Lordship online, a name you can give yourself when it's convenient (they say you get better treatment if you give yourself the title 'Lord'), and no more is required of you. Being a Christian is about becoming like Jesus. It's learning about him and getting to know him. Every day, as we know him better, we become a little more like him. And while the Holy Spirit changes us to become like Jesus, we also have to actively 'put on the new self' (4:24) – that is, to live like Christ. We have to make the choices we know God is calling us to make.

Being a Christian is full of wonderful truths, like those we have read about in the first half of Ephesians. But it's also full of practical, down-to-earth choices. Choices such as loving others, speaking truthfully, avoiding sexual sin, and treating others with respect. These are the choices we make so that the way we behave matches up with who we are in Christ.

Your old self has no hold on you, just as my old school or employers no longer have a hold on me. It's time to rebel against your old self, kick it in the shins, and run away. In the remaining chapters of Ephesians, Paul is going to give us practical choices to make, as we put on our new self. It's time to get down to business.

SOMETHING TO REFLECT ON:
Where does your new life look a lot like your old life? Where are you giving in to your 'deceitful desires'? What would it mean for you to choose to 'put on the new self'?

SOMETHING TO DO:
Spend some time in prayer, naming the areas of your life you need to hand over to Jesus, and ask him to help you put on your new self, as you look at these next chapters of Ephesians over the coming days.

A PRAYER TO PRAY:
Loving God, thank you that Jesus was willing to be put to death so that I could put to death my old self. Help me continue to embrace my new self in Jesus, so that more and more, I might become like him.

DAY TWENTY-FOUR

People of the Truth

FOCUS VERSE: EPHESIANS 4:25

READ: Ephesians 4:17–5:2

SOME THINGS TO CONSIDER:
'Stay off the grass.' 'Trespassers will be prosecuted.' 'Don't kiss the statues.' 'You must only break wind in the bathrooms provided.' How often have you seen signs like these? (Okay, maybe not quite all of these.) I feel like I see them on a semi-regular basis – in churches, at the mall, at tourist sites, in employee break rooms. I always imagine that whoever made the signs is some grumpy old person who has a very specific idea about how everyone should behave. The signs are their attempt to enforce their arbitrary preferences on everyone else because they don't trust anyone to know

how to walk on grass, respect other people's property, or fart.

If you were (or are) someone who thinks the Bible is just a book of rules, today's passage, and a lot of what's to come, is exactly what you would expect to find. It can seem like a bunch of rules from a grumpy old God who thinks we can't figure out how to live a good life on our own.

Actually, that description of God isn't totally wrong. God may not be grumpy, but he is old. Very, very old. And if he created us, he does know what's best. When you look at the way some of us stuff up our lives, it's evidence of the fact that we can't figure out the good life on our own. But the commands in chapters 4 and 5 certainly aren't about keeping us in line for arbitrary reasons. Each command is about more than just telling us how to behave: for every negative restriction, there is a positive encouragement; the commands are about helping us to have loving relationships with those around us. Remember how, up to this point in chapter 4, Paul has been encouraging the Ephesians to be unified under Jesus? Unity doesn't come through just thinking nice thoughts about other people, but through the hard work of loving each other. These rules are actually about love. The commands are the practicalities of taking off the old self and putting on the new self.

The first command is to 'put off falsehood and speak truthfully' (4:25). Why must we speak truthfully? Because God said so – it's one of the Ten Commandments. And while that is true, it's not the reason Paul gives. He says we are to be truthful people because 'we are all members

Day Twenty-four: People of the Truth

of the one body' (4:25). The relationships of Jesus' people can only function if we trust each other.

What's more, we aren't just told to be truthful to other Christians, but to our neighbour. That means everyone. Why? Again, because 'we are all members of one body'. How we behave towards people who are not Christians reflects to them what Christians are like, and by extension, what Christ is like. If Jesus is the truth, how terrible does it look if his followers lie?

I try not to lie, but when I do, it's usually because I'm afraid of what will happen if people really knew me. I lie because I want people to think I'm a better person than I am. I lie because I want people to think I do more good that I do ('If I hear a sexist joke I call it out, immediately'), or have done less bad that I have ('I have never told sexist jokes, only jokes about sexism'). My lack of truth-telling, either by outright lies, misleading information, leaving out important facts, or just not correcting a misunderstanding in my favour, all happen because I'm worried that if people knew who I really am and what I've done, they wouldn't like me.

As followers of Jesus, we know he has seen us at our worst and he knows us better than we know ourselves. Knowing us fully, he still gave his life for us, and he's not ashamed to associate with us. If Jesus can know us and love us at our worst, then we can be honest with those around us. This is easier said than done, but when we tell the truth, we are trusting others with our true self. If we are rejected because of our honesty, we're okay, because we know Jesus doesn't reject us and never will.

Trust brings the people of God together; dishonesty tears us apart. As we live truthful lives, we strengthen the body, and we point our neighbours to the King of truth who, knowing them fully, will love them too.

SOMETHING TO REFLECT ON:
What scares you most about being honest with those around you? How does the truth that Jesus knows you and loves you change how you can be honest with others?

SOMETHING TO DO:
Reflect on your last twenty-four hours. Consider when you weren't honest. What kinds of dishonesty were you most likely to engage in? Lies, misleading information, leaving facts out, not correcting misunderstandings, or something else? As you go through the next twenty-four hours, see how you can live more truthfully in one of those areas. Pay attention to how Jesus uses your honesty to make you more like him and build trust between you and others.

A PRAYER TO PRAY:
God of all truth, thank you that you know us and will never reject us. Thank you that we can always be honest with you. Help me be someone with a commitment to being truthful, for the sake of your Son and your people, even when it might cost me, just as Jesus was committed to us, even when it cost him.

DAY TWENTY-FIVE

Getting Mad

FOCUS VERSES: EPHESIANS 4:26–27

READ: Ephesians 4:17–5:2

SOME THINGS TO CONSIDER:
You could easily get the impression from Christians that anger is always wrong. Good Christians are kind, gentle, and never raise their voices. They are polite, quiet, and the worst swear words you'll hear coming out of their mouths is, 'Hell's bums!' (And even that requires some heavy duty repentance.) But if we read today's passage carefully, we see we're not told not to be angry, instead 'In your anger do not sin' (4:26). Anger is allowed. Which is good to know because to suppress your anger can be bad for your health. One study found that not

letting out your emotions can lead to early death from cancer or heart disease.[27]

Not only is bottling up your anger a bad idea, but there are some things that you should get angry about: when you see injustice, when people hurt you, or when you are confronted with sin. We should feel righteous anger about what's gone wrong in this world, but we can't let this anger lead us to lash out at others and cause more suffering. Instead, we need to deal with it in a healthy way. If we don't, we can 'give the devil a foothold' (4:27).

How do we deal healthily with anger? Paul says: 'do not let the sun go down while you are still angry' (4:26). This is not saying if you get angry just before sunset, you have only a short amount of time to be angry, or if something makes you angry just after sunset you can stay that way for almost a full twenty-four hours. What it means is we need to deal with anger quickly, because stewing on things, holding a grudge, or stuffing it down only makes it worse. If you've ever been upset with someone and couldn't get it out of your head, then you know how this can happen. Something that was a minor issue becomes huge, because you keep thinking about what was done to you, how horrible the person is who hurt you, and what you'd love to do to them if you got the chance.

So the challenge is to address the anger with the person who hurt us. When my wife gets angry at me

---

27. Benjamin P. Chapman, Kevin Fiscella, Ichiro Kawachi, Paul Duberstein, and Peter Muennig. 'Emotion Suppression and Mortality Risk over a 12-Year Follow-Up.' *Journal of Psychosomatic Research* 75, no. 4 (October 2013): 381–385. https://www.ncbi.nlm.nih.gov/pmc/articles/PMC3939772/

Day Twenty-five: Getting Mad

(usually because I've done something stupid or insensitive), she's great at telling me. She doesn't yell at me, or say mean things, she says, 'I'm annoyed at you' and then tells me why. I work hard to listen to her, to ask questions, and to not get angry in response. After these conversations, we usually both have a better idea about how we can love and care for each other.

Sometimes we can't talk to the person who hurt us, either because they are inaccessible (I can't go find the anonymous person who wrote a rude comment on my TikTok video), or maybe because we're just not ready to do it. When you've been seriously hurt, sometimes it takes longer to process what has happened. If someone burnt down your house at 9am, you don't have to be over it by 5pm. But you can start working on your anger and bringing it to God in prayer.

Not sinning in our anger is the minimum asked of us, because anger can actually lead to really good things! Anger can spur us to work at fixing what is broken in the world. Many people who fight for justice around the globe are fuelled by a righteous anger. In our personal lives, anger can help us identify where our relationships are unhealthy, and help us address those issues. Anger can also send us to God in prayer. We can pray for those people who have angered us and we can ask God to help us see how our actions might hurt others.

Anger is a huge topic to deal with, so we can't cover it all in today's devotion. But as you meditate on these verses today, remember that our best example of how to deal with anger is God himself. We know God gets angry at sin, but even though he could take it out on us, he chose to bear his judgement upon himself on the cross. His anger didn't spur him to destruction, but restoration. Our anger, if we deal with it badly, can destroy relationships and cause more pain and hurt in the world. But our anger, if used for good, can spur us to heal relationships, fight injustice, and become more like Jesus. In your anger do not sin.

SOMETHING TO REFLECT ON:
How have you seen anger used for good, either in your personal relationships or in the world?

SOMETHING TO DO:
Reflect on what is making you angry right now. Choose one positive thing you can do to use that anger to repair a relationship, or fix something that is broken in the world.

A PRAYER TO PRAY:
God of justice, thank you that instead of turning your anger upon us, you have taken it upon yourself in Jesus. May we be people who use our anger not for destruction, but for restoration.

DAY TWENTY-SIX

Takers and Givers

FOCUS VERSE: EPHESIANS 4:28

READ: Ephesians 4:17–5:2

SOME THINGS TO CONSIDER:
Once, on a Bible College ministry trip in New South Wales, me and the other students were running an event to teach local high schoolers about Jesus. The MC was using a roaming mic to ask some students if they had done anything bad lately (I'm pretty sure this was in preparation to teach them about grace; it wasn't just a public shaming event). One volunteered that they had told a lie, another that they had been mean to their brother. Then a girl put up her hand to say that she and her friends had stolen a car on the weekend. The poor Christian MC didn't know what

to say! He had not been expecting public confessions of crimes.

In today's passage, Paul's instruction to the Ephesian churches is quite simply that people who have been stealing should stop. And this tells us something important about the people who were in these churches. Not only were there well-behaved people but also thieves. The girl who stole a car would have fitted right in![28]

Now my guess is that most of you reading this are not car thieves (though if you are one – hello! Is it true you can use a screwdriver to start a car?), but perhaps we have been known to partake in some other more 'respectable' ways to steal – torrenting, sharing logins, slacking off at work, spending money on our parents' credit card without their knowledge. And to all thieves, what does Paul say? Stop it.

Because stealing, which makes clear the state of our hearts, shows our sense of entitlement. My guess is, most of us who steal things don't do it because we're starving and need a loaf of bread to feed our family. Instead, we think we deserve whatever we desire. It also shows our lack of trust in God. We don't trust God to give us what we need and what is best, so we take it for ourselves. When we choose honesty, we choose to trust God's provision.

What does Paul suggest we do instead of stealing? Work. And not because it keeps you out or trouble, or makes you respectable, but so that through your work

---

28. This isn't part of the big idea of this devotion, but it may be worth considering if she would fit in at your youth group or church. Would she be just as welcome as the kid whose worst sin is telling a lie or being mean to their sibling? If not, how do you think your community might need to change so she would be welcome? Okay, you can go back the to main devotion now.

Day Twenty-six: Takers and Givers

you can have something to give to those in need. Instead of taking from our community, work allows us to give to it. Instead of taking from others because we don't trust God to provide, we give to others as an act of trust in God's provision. You could do this through giving to charities who help those who are in need, or you can do it in informal ways like cooking meals for people who are sick, or giving money to friends who might be struggling. My wife and I put money aside every time we get paid, not just to give to the church, but also to give to anyone in need who we might come across.

Being someone who gives rather than takes doesn't mean you have to wait until you get a job. You can still choose to be someone who works to give to those around you. You have time, friendships, and maybe some cash from pocket money or doing odd jobs. You have the ability to volunteer with your church or a charity, visit people who are lonely, or use your creativity to write songs, make videos, or create some art to bless your community.

Something wonderful about being a Christian is that we can see this principle worked out in the life of Jesus. Jesus, as God, deserves all things. Every thing, and every person, rightfully belongs to him. And yet, instead of taking what he deserved, he gave us what we do not deserve. He trusted his Father that he would rise again when he gave up his life for those who were in need. Now, as we live in the power of his resurrection, we can live a generous life for Jesus marked by giving rather than taking, albeit in a small way, doing what he has already done for us.

SOMETHING TO REFLECT ON:
Are you taking what is not yours to take? What resources do you have available that you can share with those in need?

SOMETHING TO DO:
As you consider what you have that you can give, take one practical step today to give to someone who is in need.

A PRAYER TO PRAY:
Generous God, thank you that Jesus did not hoard what he had for himself, but willingly gave up his life so that we might become yours. Help me see that just as Jesus trusted in you that he would rise again, I can trust you to provide what I need as I give what I have to those who are in need.

DAY TWENTY-SEVEN
F-bombs and Other Weapons of Mass Destruction

FOCUS VERSE: EPHESIANS 4:29

READ: Ephesians 4:17–5:2

SOME THINGS TO CONSIDER:
As I write this, the Olympic Games are on TV. My wife has promised to tell me any time an Australian is competing for a medal. She just called me to come and watch the women's 100 metres backstroke final. It was lucky she did because the Australian just won gold and broke the Olympic record in the process. It was very exciting!

In her post-match interview, the Australian swimmer was so excited that she dropped an F-bomb, before quickly covering her mouth. It was pretty funny – and also fortuitous, because I'm in the middle of writing this devotion about the things that come out of our mouths.

I was obsessed by the Olympics as a kid. Had I seen that interview as a nine-year-old, it would have scandalised me. I thought swearing was one of the worst things a kid could do. Of course, I knew that there were worse things in the world, but stealing the world's largest diamond, for instance, seemed like a pretty inaccessible sin for a good Christian kid like me.[29]

When Christians want a justification for why we shouldn't use coarse language, we turn to this verse, as if it's the knock-down-drag-out verse for not dropping f-bombs. Or any type of single-letter-bomb. But is this verse actually about swearing? It's not as if any of the swear words we hear today were around when Ephesians was written. Let me put it this way: it's not not about swearing, but it is about a whole lot more than swearing. It's about not gossiping, insulting and putting others down, gaslighting, using our words to manipulate or gain power over others, or saying anything that might be unhelpful. The winning swimmer's celebratory swearing, while I wouldn't encourage it in church, didn't tear down or abuse anyone, it was a release of unbridled happiness. But there are plenty of things Christians say which might not involve coarse language but do do terrible damage to

---

29. That's not to say that I wouldn't have planned how to steal a jewel as a kid – I spent a lot of time planning crimes as a child. Not because I was going to commit them, I should add, they just seemed like fun problems to solve.

Day Twenty-seven: F-bombs and Other Weapons of Mass Destruction

others. James tells us that when we insult others, we insult the image of God, as each person is made in his image (James 3:9).

The problem is, it's so easy to say words without thinking, especially around people we are comfortable with, like our family and friends. Unfortunately, it's extremely hard to undo the consequences. The words we say can be like a small spark that starts a huge fire (see James 3:1–12). Our careless words can leave lasting wounds on the lives of others.

Chances are you can recall hurtful things people have said to you, that they have long forgotten. But likewise, you can probably recall kind, encouraging words that others have said to you, that they have also long forgotten. The positive outcome of our words is that we can build others up with them. If we only sought to say things that were a benefit to everyone who was listening (and those our words could get back to), imagine how much good we could do. If Christians only spoke in love about and to each other, imagine how much more unified we'd be – the very thing Paul is so concerned about.

I once had a youth leader who encouraged us to be good gossips. To say kind things about others behind their backs. I loved that idea, so I stole it, and I've been encouraging people to do it ever since. It feels great when someone tells me that a parent at my youth group was talking about me and saying how thankful they are for me.

Also, when we choose to 'not let any unwholesome talk come out of [our] mouths' we stand out. When our conversation only builds others up, people notice. One of the most effective ways we can show that we belong to Jesus is with our words.

Words can seem like a small thing, but they really matter. There is a reason the Bible teaches us that God created the world with just the words he spoke (Genesis 1), or describes Jesus as the Word made flesh (John 1). It's because our words have immense power for evil or for good. The words that God says about us change who we are. You only have to look back at the amazing things we learn about our identity in Christ, written in the words of Ephesians, to see how powerful God's word is in building us up. May we all harness the power of our words, for the good of everyone they may affect.

SOMETHING TO REFLECT ON:
When are you most likely to use unhelpful words? How can you reflect the love of God, and the value of others, in the words you say? How will you create good in this world with your powerful words?

SOMETHING TO DO:
Today, see if you can do two things: do good gossip behind someone's back, and apologise to someone's face for unhelpful things you have said about them.

A PRAYER TO PRAY:
God, whose word is always true and good, help me reflect your life-giving power in the way I use my words. Give me self-control to not say the hurtful things I want to, and a heart of love and courage to say what will build others up.

DAY TWENTY-EIGHT

The Sad Spirit

FOCUS VERSE: EPHESIANS 4:30

READ: Ephesians 4:17–5:2

SOME THINGS TO CONSIDER:
Is there a worse feeling in the world than making someone cry? If there is, I don't know what it is.[30] A little while ago, I took my four-year-old nephew swimming. On our way back from the pool, while wrapped in a towel, he tried to negotiate the entrance to our apartment building. In doing so, he tripped over the door ledge, fell flat on his face, and started crying. As I picked him up, he said, 'You should have carried

---

30. There probably *are* worse feelings in the world, like perhaps making someone cry while simultaneously amputating your own leg without anaesthetic. But seeing as I have never done that, we'll just stick with making someone cry.

Ephesians

me! You should have carried me!' And then cried all the more. I felt pretty bad.

Today's instruction is not to grieve the Holy Spirit, that is, don't make the Holy Spirit sad.[31] Happily, the Holy Spirit is not like a small boy who we neglect to help and make cry. But what do we do that saddens the Holy Spirit? If you read this verse in isolation, you'd have no idea. You could spend your whole life worried that you're grieving the Holy Spirit. But, as you may have noticed, we're not reading this verse in isolation. We're twenty-eight days into Ephesians, so hopefully we have a fair idea of what has come before. Right before this verse is yesterday's instruction to make sure we don't use unwholesome talk. Is it this that grieves the Holy Spirit? Does he have delicate sensitivities that can't handle vulgar language? No, but remember how at the beginning of chapter 4, Paul was banging on about unity? Nothing destroys unity among God's people quicker than us speaking badly about others. Gossip, bullying, snide remarks, complaining, and rude outbursts, these will eat away at the unity of the church. Our mouths cause more damage to the work of Jesus than pretty much anything else.[32] So when Christians use unkind words about each other, it saddens the Holy Spirit because it undermines the unity he has given us.

Keeping from unwholesome talk isn't the only instruction we've recently read. As we put on our new self

---

31. As an important aside, if the Holy Spirit can be grieved, then it's clear that the Spirit is not an impersonal force, but a person with feelings who can be affected by the behaviour of humans. While the phrase 'the Trinity' is not found anywhere in the Bible, this verse is one of the key pieces of evidence that there are three persons in our one God.

32. I have no scientific basis for this claim, it's just a vibe I've got.

Day Twenty-eight: The Sad Spirit

(4:24), we are to get rid of lying, sinful anger, and stealing (4:25–28). These behaviours also grieve the Holy Spirit because of how they affect our relationships with others, and our relationship with him. And so we choose to live differently because we belong to Jesus. That is what it means to be 'sealed for the day of redemption' (4:30) – we live obediently now because we belong to Jesus knowing one day he is coming back for us.

That our behaviour can grieve the Holy Spirit shows us that obeying God is not just a matter of keeping some arbitrary laws and ticking a few boxes. We are living out our faith in relationship with others and with God. Obedience is personal, it affects our relationship with God and others. If breaking his laws grieves him, then obeying them will bring him joy. It's like the difference between not putting your feet on the seat of the train or walking through Mum's veggie patch. You might get fined for putting your feet on seats, but the government will not feel personally upset. But if your mum has a bunch of carrots and parsley growing in the front yard and you go stomp on them, you won't get fined, but she is going to be pretty sad that you disrespected her like that. Our obedience flows from our relationship with God. In the same way, insulting or hurting people created in his image hurts him.

This verse could be used to guilt us into being good people, but I think we should look at it another way. Not wanting to grieve the Spirit should spur us on to not hurting or abusing others. We can let the positives of this verse encourage us: as we love and care for others, speaking kindly about them, and building them up with our words, we can delight the Holy Spirit. Let's be people who bring joy to our God because of how we care for others.

SOMETHING TO REFLECT ON:
How does an awareness that your actions affect the emotions of the Holy Spirit spur you on to love and care for those around you?

SOMETHING TO DO:
Make it your mission today to delight the Holy Spirit. As you encounter others, seek opportunities to treat them with kindness and love, knowing that you are bringing happiness to your God.

A PRAYER TO PRAY:
God who cares, thank you that you are not an impersonal deity, but that you are emotionally invested in your people. Please forgive me for the way I have grieved your Holy Spirit in the past. Please help me care for those around me and live in a way that delights you.

DAY TWENTY-NINE

The Example

FOCUS VERSES: EPHESIANS 4:31–5:2

READ: Ephesians 4:18–5:2

SOME THINGS TO CONSIDER:
'Because I said so!'

These are infamous words that have come out of the mouths of many exasperated parents. When a kid asks why they should brush their teeth, put on their shoes, or not set the cat on fire, the parent snaps: 'Because I said so!' It is the authority that parents hold that means their kids are obedient. But as soon the kid realises that their parents aren't all-powerful, and they have their own, better ideas about how to govern their life, all bets are off.

Sometimes we treat the commands in the Bible the same way. Why shouldn't I fly into a rage, or speak badly about others? Because God said so. Of course, if anyone has the authority to tell us to do something and expect us to do it, it's God. But as we continually see throughout Ephesians, and the Bible, God is not arbitrary in his commands. He doesn't just expect us to obey him blindly. He only asks us to go where he has gone before. That's what makes today's passage so special. It shows us the explicit connection between how we love others and how God has loved us. What starts as a command to not indulge in destructive anger becomes a reflection on the sacrifice of Jesus.

You may wonder, as you read the passage, why we're told to get rid of all anger, when back in verse 26 anger was allowed if we did not sin? Is Paul contradicting himself? It may seem that way, but look at the context of what Paul is saying. He uses anger and five other words for hateful human relations, and none of them are good. Rage and brawling imply an anger that is let loose on people. Slander is a way of speaking untruthfully about others to cause maximum damage. Bitterness and malice carry the poison of hatred. Put all these words together and Paul is not talking about a productive anger that leads you to seek a more just world, or restore a relationship, but a destructive, uncontrolled anger that seeks only to hurt and destroy those who get in its way.

So what are we called to instead? Kindness, compassion, and forgiveness. These things are the opposite of uncontrolled anger. Instead of flying into a rage, we can choose to act with kindness, even towards those who anger us. Instead of spreading lies about others and destroying

Day Twenty-nine: The Example

their reputation, we can seek to understand their situation and what may have caused them to act in ways that upset us. Instead of harbouring bitterness and malice, we can choose to let go of our right for retribution and forgive those who have hurt us.

This all sounds nice in theory until you have to do it. Then it's just really hard and promises little reward or satisfaction. It certainly won't give you the immediate satisfaction of putting someone on blast. So why would you do it? Not because it's some arbitrary command of God, but because Jesus did it for us.

All the commands in this letter are about following Jesus' example of love. If we look at the way Jesus lived, he shows us what a life full of kindness, compassion, forgiveness, and even constructive anger looks like. His love was so deep he demonstrated it by going to the cross on our behalf, even while we were enemies of God. There is no better reason to live a life of kindness, compassion, and forgiveness than because we want to walk in the footsteps of Jesus.

Paul's talk about Jesus' sacrifice being a 'fragrant offering' (5:2) may seem like weird language, but he's referencing the Old Testament. There, descriptions of animal and food sacrifices made by God's people in worship are often described as a 'pleasing aroma' for God. Jesus' death is the ultimate sacrifice, which all other sacrifices point to.

Now, as we live lives of love, we are worshipping God with our own sacrifices. Not of animals or food, but with our lives. We are, as Paul describes elsewhere, living sacrifices (Romans 12:1). This giving up of anger, and choosing instead to love, may cost us, but we are following the example of God, who paid everything to love us. There is no better reason to obey. We are kind, because he is kind. We are compassionate, because he has compassion. We forgive, because he forgives. We love, because he loves. God's justification for our obedience is never 'because I said so', but always 'because I did so'.

SOMETHING TO REFLECT ON:
What does it mean to you that Jesus never asks us to do something he hasn't already done himself? How does that change how you choose to live?

SOMETHING TO DO:
Is there anyone in your life who you have a broken relationship with because of your anger? Take a step today to repair that relationship, choosing kindness, compassion, and forgiveness, even though it might cost you.

A PRAYER TO PRAY:
God who goes before us, thank you that you are our perfect example. Thank you that Jesus shows us what a life of love looks like, and his sacrifice empowers us to live that life. May I follow in the footsteps of Jesus, and be willing to love sacrificially, even when I may want to do the opposite.

DAY THIRTY

The One About Sex

FOCUS VERSE: EPHESIANS 5:3A

READ: Ephesians 5:3–20

SOME THINGS TO CONSIDER:
My primary school had a tradition of running a session on puberty for every year five student. One night, we all had to go to school with a parent to watch a video about hair growing in funny places and the mechanics of baby-making.

After this horrifying experience (I think having to be at school outside of school hours was worse than the animated sperm movie), my dad took me out for a thickshake at Maccas. There, he asked me if I had any questions. 'Nope,' I said, probably much to his relief, and we got on with drinking our thickshakes.

Sex is one of those topics that we love talking about and are also super awkward talking about. Sometimes it might feel like we Christians talk about it not enough and too much, all at the same time.

Here, Paul isn't shying away from sex, but he clearly isn't caught up on it either. It's half a sentence in the whole letter. But the command is pretty far-reaching. 'There must not be even a hint of sexual immorality.' He doesn't say 'just avoid the big sexual sins', but avoid anything that even looks like it might be wrong.

Sexual immorality is a broad term for any sexual act that falls outside of the committed, loving marriage of a man and woman.[33] That includes sex with anyone you're not married to, pornography, lust, sexual harassment, and lots more.

Unfortunately, since the days of the Bible, this has been one of the hardest commands for Christians to keep. You only have to scratch the surface of church scandals to see that there has been way more than a hint of sexual immorality. And it has been those scandals

---

33. I'm aware that some readers will be concerned that this definition doesn't accommodate same-sex couples. If that's you, please don't switch off or give up on these devotions. I think we can disagree on these things and still love Jesus. While there isn't space to discuss homosexuality here, if you would like to read a book that pretty much encapsulates my position, check out *A People to be Loved: Why Homosexuality is Not Just an Issue* by Preston Sprinkle (Grand Rapids: Zondervan, 2015).

And if you are someone who is gay or same-sex attracted with a different view of sexuality to me, please do not let one sentence from me (and the countless terrible and thoughtless things Christians have said and done) turn you off Jesus. The most important thing is to discover Jesus' love for you. Everything else you can figure out later. And even if you and I think differently about issues of sexuality, Jesus' love can cover that too. Let's both seek to be faithful to Jesus, and go wherever that leads.

Day Thirty: The One About Sex

that have caused some of the most damage to the cause of Christ.

When you're young, sex can be an especially big deal. Not because old people have sex all figured out, but because Christian young people are in a perfect storm of a newly developing sex drive, raging hormones, a lack of experience, a sexualised culture, a desire to explore, and no place to explore before they're married. Back when Ephesians was written, people would get married as teenagers, so they wouldn't have to wait nearly so long for biblically faithful sex, but in those times people often had arranged marriages with their cousins, so I'm not sure we really want to go back there.

So how do you make sure there is not even a hint of sexual immorality in your life, even when you're dealing with all the issues you face as a young person? We're certainly not going to cover everything there is to cover about sex in one devotion, but perhaps this might be a good place to begin figuring stuff out.

Some tips to avoid sexual immorality:

Get educated – Too many people learn about sex through porn. This is like trying to learn how to drive a car by watching *The Fast and the Furious* movies. It's unrealistic, and if you try it, you're going to do a lot of damage to yourself and those around you.[34] Instead, make sure you take the time to learn about sex from

---

34. When I wrote this I thought I was really smart, but it turns out that I stole it from Jameela Jamil who said something very similar way before I wrote anything down: https://www.yahoo.com/lifestyle/may-fight-generation-men-read-jameela-jamils-powerful-speech-ending-toxic-masculinity-235720491.html

wise Christians, read some good books, and follow some great Christian sex education accounts on social media.[35]

Talk about sex – One of the big reasons we have so many issues with sexual sin is because we don't talk about sex. When we don't talk about sex, we can feel like the most terrible, depraved people. Talking about sex can help us realise we're not alone in our struggles, and we can have our questions answered in a healthy way. When we ask questions, share our struggles, and confess our sin, we are in a much better position to get the support we need when we slip up. The people we talk to can remind us that sexual sin, while still sin, is not the most terrible of all sins. They can give us the right perspective and remind us of God's unlimited forgiveness and grace. The people you might like to talk to are your parents (if it's not too weird), a youth pastor or youth leader, and even your Christian friends.

Focus on the gospel – Perhaps the biggest problem with the way we talk about sex is that we forget how important God made it to be. As we'll see later in Ephesians 5, marriage is a picture of Jesus' love for his Church. The way a husband and wife give themselves to each other is a picture of the love Jesus has for us. Sex is a bodily giving of yourself to another person. In Jesus' life, death, and resurrection, Jesus gives all of himself on our behalf. Sex is more than just a physical act, and it's more than just

---

35. Some recommendations are: John Mark Comer, *Loveology: God, Love, Marriage, Sex and the Never-Ending Story of Male and Female* (Grand Rapids: Zondervan, 2013); Patricia Weerakoon, *Teen Sex by the Book* (Sydney South: Anglican Youthworks, 2013); @BigKidsTable on Instagram.

Day Thirty: The One About Sex

something that happens between two people, in the right context, it is a testament to the greatest act of self-giving love in history.

As you seek to live a sexually faithful life, remember you aren't just keeping some arbitrary rules, you are living a life of faithful witness to the all-giving love that Jesus has for us.

SOMETHING TO REFLECT ON:
Where could there be a hint (or more) of sexual immorality in your life? How may God be convicting you to live faithfully for him?

SOMETHING TO DO:
Find someone to talk to or begin getting yourself educated about what faithfulness to Jesus looks like with regards to sex.

A PRAYER TO PRAY:
Faithful God, thank you that Jesus shows us what faithful, self-giving love looks like. Please give me the strength and courage to live a life free from sexual immorality, even if that requires significant sacrifice.

DAY THIRTY-ONE

Showing Up

FOCUS VERSES: EPHESIANS 5:3–7

READ: Ephesians 5:3–20

SOME THINGS TO CONSIDER:
I once worked part-time as an usher at a 13,000-seat arena. This meant I got to see lots of famous bands play their shows, as well as endure many boring conferences. Along with checking tickets and opening doors for people, my job also entailed herding drunk people who couldn't find their seats and trying not to get beaten up by aggressive concert-goers.

    I eventually got another, full-time, job, but I kept the ushering job so I could keep seeing shows and earn a little more money. But whenever the schedule got emailed out with new events to usher at, I'd look at the times and feel too lazy to sign up for any. After nine months of this, I got a letter informing me I was fired. This was fair enough. Employees should probably work for their employer. Unfortunately for me, I still had a belt and a pair of shoes in my locker, which I never got back. Life can be tough.

Today's passage raises a question: can you get fired from being a Christian? Of course, we're not employees of Jesus, but we read that there are some people who won't have 'any inheritance in the kingdom of Christ and of God'. These are people who are 'immoral, impure or greedy' (5:5).

Paul warned us yesterday against having even a hint of sexual immorality. If we have more than a hint, are we the immoral people Paul is writing about?

What about being impure? We sully our purity not just through sexual immorality but through any kind of sinful living that rejects the purity of obedience to God for the impurity of gratifying our own sinful desires.

What about greed? Greed is about taking more for yourself than you are entitled to. In relation to sexual immorality, when a person lusts after another, when they look at pornography, when they sexually abuse someone, this is greed. They take what is not theirs for their own satisfaction. I keep coming back to sex, because it set the theme of the passage by kicking off the paragraph, but what about beyond sex? If, like me, you live in a wealthy Western country, you most likely have more wealth than most of humanity, you consume more than your fair share of the world's resources, and your lifestyle emits more

Day Thirty-one: Showing Up

carbon than your less wealthy neighbours'. This is our society's greed, which destroys lives and benefits us. So if we have ever taken more than our fair share, are we destined for judgement?

This passage is not saying that people who have been immoral, impure, or greedy cannot be saved. It is saying that people may say they follow Jesus, but if they live immoral, impure, or greedy lives, they are actually in rebellion against God.

When I said I was an usher but refused to take shifts, I wasn't really an usher, and I deserved to be fired. Someone who says they love Jesus, but embraces sexual immorality, lives an impure life. Someone who hoards wealth for themselves, without regard for those who are in need, doesn't truly love Jesus. These people are idolators because they love their sin more than they love God.

Jesus teaches, 'If you love me, keep my commands' (John 14:15). Our love is proved through our actions, and our faith shows itself as genuine by how we live. The person who is living constantly in rebellion against God, ignoring his commands, does not love him, and cannot inherit his kingdom unless they repent. However, if we are working to live a more obedient life with God's help, even if we sometimes get it wrong, God will not reject us. Our actions show where our true love lies.

Unfortunately, we live in a time when people preach easy grace. They tell us that God loves us and asks for nothing in return. In this religion, God will save even those in open rebellion against him and call it tolerance. But Paul disagrees. He wants the churches to know that if someone keeps going against God, God will not force them into his kingdom, under his rule. If you want to live in rebellion, then God won't impose his kingdom on you. You can choose to live free of God, but you will also live free of the benefits of the kingdom.

There's a lot more we could say about this short passage (we didn't even touch on filthy language – have a look back at Day Twenty-seven if you want a speech refresher). But for now, let's leave it at this: the challenge of these verses is to keep up the fight against immorality, impurity, and greed. No one slips into a holy life, but it's easy to slide into sin. Jesus' death saves us from being punished for our sin, and it saves us from having to continue to live in our sin. We worship Jesus as God, not only through our words but through living the way he calls us to. As citizens of his kingdom, we live out our love with our actions.

SOMETHING TO REFLECT ON:
In what area of your life – immorality, impurity, greed, or even your speech – do you think Jesus might be calling you to greater obedience? What might it look like to show your love for him by obeying his commands?

SOMETHING TO DO:
Keeping in mind your reflections, write on a piece of paper one word to remind yourself of what you would like to be working on to obey Jesus. Stick that piece of paper somewhere you will see it every day to remind you to obey Jesus in this area.

A PRAYER TO PRAY:
Lord God, help me live with you as God of all my life. May I show my love for you not just in the words I say but in the way I live as a citizen of your kingdom.

DAY THIRTY-TWO

Living Light

FOCUS VERSES: EPHESIANS 5:8-14

READ: Ephesians 5:3-20

SOME THINGS TO CONSIDER:
Have you ever arrived at a holiday destination in the dark? You pull up at your accommodation after a long drive. Unlocking the door with the key that's been left out, you drag your bags into the cold, unfamiliar place. Then you walk around, turning on lights, scoping it out, trying to figure out which bed is the best and making sure you get it for yourself. Pretty soon, you've done your teeth, you're in your pjs, and you're tucked up in an unfamiliar bed hoping you don't sleep too badly and wondering about all the strange things that might be just outside your front door.

In the morning, you get up and look out the window and see a magnificent view. You missed it the night before because you arrived in the dark. Perhaps your accommodation looks straight out on the vast ocean with waves breaking gently on the beach, or maybe there is a green field covered in mist, sitting at the foot of imposing cliffs with the rising sun reflecting off them. What vistas have you woken up to, that you never saw in the dark?

This contrast between what you experience in the night and during the day is what Paul is drawing on in this passage. He is telling his readers not that we were once in darkness, but that we actually were darkness. We weren't merely deceived by sin, or dabbling in sin, but we were full participants in it – so much so that darkness became our identity. As it says in 2:3: 'we were by nature deserving of wrath'. But now we have been completely transformed by Jesus, so that we are as different from our old self as light is to darkness.

If we really have been transformed, the challenge then is to live as transformed people. All these commands that we have been reading are expressions of our new identity. Our behaviour should match our status. Being a follower of Jesus must change how we live. The difference between our life as a Christian and our life as a non-believer should be as stark as night and day. When we get saved, we don't stay the same but with slightly better morals and slightly less cool friends. We should allow Jesus to transform everything about how we live. Our lives are to be characterised by 'goodness, righteousness and truth' (5:9).

Day Thirty-two: Living Light

A transformed life means total transformation – we should have nothing to do with the deeds of darkness. It means that the way we treat our friends and our family should look radically different from the way we would treat them if we didn't know Jesus – like night and day. The way we love others, the way we date, the way we behave playing sport or at a party, the things we say and do online – everything should be filled with light. If someone were to look at our life, our faith in Jesus shouldn't be ambiguous. We can't be kind and pleasant at church, but horrible at home and manipulative with our friends. Jesus' love should shine through in every part of our lives.

There is more to being 'children of the light' than having nothing to do with the deeds of darkness. Just as light transforms darkness, our lives should be transformed and transformative (5:13). In the broad sense, this is the work that Jesus does in our lives: our sin is made clear to us and we grow to be more like him. And as we are light in the world, we will also transform the world. When we bring the love of Jesus to those around us, not only will the truth be made known but people will put their faith in Jesus too! As we are faithful to Jesus we cannot help but transform the lives of those around us.

This is a massive and important calling. As the final verse of today's passage says, it's time to wake up and take hold of our new life. When we've been saved by Jesus, it is like we have awoken in a new world. Not just at a holiday destination, but with a whole new life – a transformed character, forgiven and empowered by the Spirit to live for Jesus and transform the world with his light.

SOMETHING TO REFLECT ON:
Who do you know whose life is light? How do you see the fruit of goodness, righteousness, and truth transforming their life and the lives of those around them?

SOMETHING TO DO:
Spend some time in prayer asking God if there are any areas of your life where you have been engaged in 'deeds of darkness'. Let his conviction and light begin to transform how you live in that area.

A PRAYER TO PRAY:
God of light, thank you that you do not make us slightly better people, but you completely transform our identity. Please empower me with your Spirit so that the way I live matches who I am. May the way I live bring your light into the lives of those around me, too.

DAY THIRTY-THREE

Live for the Moment

FOCUS VERSES: EPHESIANS 5:15–21

READ: Ephesians 5:3–21

SOME THINGS TO CONSIDER:
'Live for the moment!', 'Seize the day!', 'Don't wait for tomorrow. Do it now!' You could find these phrases featuring in badly designed Instagram quotes or printed on cushions in a cheap furniture store. You might not expect a similar quote to pop up in Ephesians, but in this passage, I feel like we're almost at cushion-quote level. '[Make] the most of every opportunity, because the days are evil' (5:16) may not be as peppy we'd like, but Paul is mining the same vein of 'live for the moment' sentiment as those other popular quotes. What is important is how we do that. Living for the moment may result in reckless

behaviour, but Paul is asking God's people to do the opposite. The way to make the most of every opportunity is not to just do the most exciting thing possible or follow your feelings to an 'authentic life'; it's wise living. Why? Because the days are evil.

You only have to look at how humans treat each other, or feel the ever-growing threat of climate change, to see that we live in evil days. Right now, evil appears to reign and Satan is having his way. One day, Jesus will return and put the world right. That is good news, but it means we have limited time to bring the light of Christ to those living in darkness. So we must make the most of every opportunity through wise living.

What is wise living? It is understanding what the Lord's will is (5:17). Look back at chapter 1 and you'll see Paul teaching that God's will is to rescue a people for himself (1:4–5). In the big picture, life is not about making ourselves rich, famous, comfortable, or secure. It's about living in response to a God who has predestined us for salvation, for his glory. This is wise living, and it changes how we behave each day.

One of the clearest examples of living for the moment is the fleeting happiness of getting drunk. Paul teaches the Ephesian churches not to get drunk on wine (or beer, spirits, or cheap alcohol that you convinced some adult to buy for you, or the stuff you stole from your parent's stash) but by being filled with the Holy Spirt (5:18). Being drunk affects your self-control, judgement, physical abilities, and wisdom. The Holy Spirit gives you self-control, helps your judgement, and gives you wisdom.

Day Thirty-three: Live for the Moment

He is the opposite of alcohol.

What, then, does it mean to be filled with the Spirit? This is the perfect passage to clear up any confusion about what being 'Spirit-filled' is, and it's got nothing to do with waving flags in worship (but feel free to do it if that's your thing). Being filled with the Spirit is about speaking and singing, giving thanks, and submitting (5:19–21).

Spirit-filled people speak to each other 'with psalms, hymns, and songs from the Spirit', and singing and making music to the Lord (5:19). This doesn't mean we only communicate through songs like we're in some kind of Christian musical. It means we make praising God through music a regular part of our time with other Christians. As we sing either in formal settings like church services, or informal ones like a road trip singalong, we paise Jesus. We can even pepper our conversations with references to the songs we all know to encourage each other on in our faith.

Spirit-filled followers also live a life of thanksgiving (5:20). This doesn't mean that we must thank God for absolutely everything, as if everything is good. You don't have to thank God for stubbing your toe, getting bullied, or for diarrhoea. But we always have things to thank God for – our salvation, God's kindness, Jesus' sacrifice, the coming new creation – as well as the temporal things like our breakfast, our family and friends, our schooling, and video streaming services, to name just a few. Remembering the good gifts God has given us will transform how we experience unpleasant things, like stubbing our toes, being bullied, and diarrhoea. They won't be the catastrophes they sometimes feel like because God's goodness is always in our hearts and minds.

Finally, Spirit-filled people submit to each other 'out of reverence for Christ' (5:21). Over the next few days, we will look at what it means to submit to each other in the various relationships that we have. But in short, being in Christ means we don't have to assert ourselves to be the most important person in any situation. We can be content to put others before ourselves and seek their good because Christ has done that for us. The Spirit-filled Christian doesn't need to be the alpha to know that they matter.

So what does Paul mean when he says to seize the moment? He means we should live wisely, filled with the Spirit, praising God and encouraging each other, living with thankfulness, and submitting to each other. This may not seem as exciting as blowing all your money on a tattoo while skydiving in Dubai, but it's certainly going to be a more sustainable, life-giving way to live as we wait for Jesus to return and end these evil days.

SOMETHING TO REFLECT ON:
What might God be calling you to do to live wisely? Does it have to do with alcohol, praise, thanksgiving, or submitting? What does your Spirit-filled life look like?

SOMETHING TO DO:
Depending how you answered the above questions, consider how you can rely on the Spirit to empower you to live a more Spirit-filled life in the area you need to focus on.

Day Thirty-three: Live for the Moment

A PRAYER TO PRAY:

Holy Spirt, please fill me, so that I can become more like Jesus, sing and speak his praises, live in thankfulness, and submit to others. Help me live wisely, making the most of the time you have given me.

DAY THIRTY-FOUR
Relationship Revolution

FOCUS VERSES: EPHESIANS 5:21–33

READ: Ephesians 5:21–6:9

SOME THINGS TO CONSIDER:
In 2009, while I was sitting on a roof, my old Nokia phone died. 'Excellent!' I thought. 'This is my excuse to finally get an iPhone.' So I went to the shops and got my first iPhone. It was amazing! So shiny! So fancy! With its cutting edge technology and design, it was a revolution compared to the Nokia brick I had been using. But if I fired up that iPhone today, I know that while there are some things that would still feel familiar, there would be a lot of things that now feel as clunky and outdated as my Nokia did.

As we read this passage about marriage in our context, some parts can sound wonderful and revolutionary. Other parts feel outdated and incompatible with the way we do relationships today. As we look at these verses, however, it's important to remember the context it was written in. When Ephesians was written, wives were viewed as the possession of their husbands. Husbands were not expected to love their wives, or treat them well. Wives could be compelled to obedience by abusive husbands, and no one would think twice about it.

So imagine reading this letter as a first-century Christian and hearing husbands shouldn't rule over nor control their wives. They shouldn't even be indifferent to their wives. The Christian husband must treat his wife not like someone foisted upon him by his family (many marriages were arranged), but he must choose to love her. He must choose the same love that Jesus has for us. Love that is willing to die for his wife, and love that is willing to put his wife first in everything. That is a revolution!

Wives, on the other hand, were in a different situation. They had little power. Now, because of the gospel, women were to be treated as equal members of God's family. How would they use their new status and freedom? By leaving their husbands? Or seeking to aggressively overturn the power imbalance they had lived with? No. They were asked to submit to their husbands. Their submission was not to be forced upon them by their husbands, but Paul asked them to choose to do it.

Why? Because marriage, far from being a contract to enhance a family's social standing, or a loveless power

Day Thirty-four: Relationship Revolution

struggle within which children were created, was to be a picture of how much God loves us (5:31–32). Paul showed how marriage is a living illustration of Jesus' relationship with the Church. As husbands sacrificially loved their wives, and wives lovingly submitted to their husbands, they were revolutionising marriage. How Christians treated each other, even within marriage, would show the world a picture of how committed Jesus is to us, and we can respond to his love.

Can you see how revolutionary that change to marriage might have been in the ancient world? How amazing that a husband and wife who love and submit to each other would be a living testament to the love of Jesus?

These days, like my 2009 iPhone, some features of an Ephesians 5 marriage may seem outdated. And, don't you worry, there is plenty of debate about exactly what these verses mean in practice today. But what they can't mean is that modern Christian marriage should be less than what Paul describes here. Like how the iPhone keeps being improved, Christians should continue to be leaders in revolutionarily loving marriages. We should keep discovering more ways to submit to each other out of reverence for Christ (5:21). We should have marriages that reflect Jesus' sacrificial love, not asserting power and control over the other person, but giving up power and serving, because that is what Jesus has done for us.

There is plenty more to be said about submission, husbands as the head, and sacrificial love, but I won't cover that here because there isn't the time or space to deal with everything in this passage with the nuance, gentleness, and generosity needed for a controversial topic like this.[36] What I will say is, whatever position a Christian takes on these questions, it must be one that leads to marriages that are more loving, more sacrificial, and more gentle, kind, and patient than those of the surrounding culture. They must leave no room for abuse or control. Any Christian view of marriage that leaves room for behaviour like this is not Christian at all, because that is never how Jesus treats us.

But now let's think about what it means for you, right now. If you're reading this, and you're in my target demographic, you're a teenager, so you're probably not married. But that doesn't mean this passage is irrelevant. As you think about the relationships that you do have, how can you make them little pictures of Jesus' love? How can you submit to others, because you know Jesus submitted himself to his father? How can you love other people even when it costs you? How can you live in Jesus' transforming power each day, so that if you become a husband or wife, you will be prepared to reflect Jesus' love in how you treat the person you are married to? And how can you revolutionise your relationships right now so that how you treat others tells of the story of how Jesus has treated us?

---

[36]. I'm sure that for some of you this will feel like a cop out. You may want me to come down firmly on one side or the other of the debate over exactly what these verses mean. If that's you, then until I say otherwise, just assume that I agree with you and we can all get along swimmingly.

Day Thirty-four: Relationship Revolution

SOMETHING TO REFLECT ON:
What marriages have you seen that best reflect Jesus' love for us? What is it about those marriages that stand out to you as showing Jesus' love?

SOMETHING TO DO:
Think of someone in a marriage you admire. Text them and ask them for one piece of advice to become someone who reflects Jesus in all your relationships.

A PRAYER TO PRAY:
Loving God, thank you that you have shown us your love in Jesus. Thank you that he does not oppress or control us, but gave himself up for us. Transform me by your Spirit so that in all my relationships, I will better reflect Jesus' love for us.

DAY THIRTY-FIVE
Parents Can Be Exasperating

FOCUS VERSES: EPHESIANS 6:1-4

READ: Ephesians 5:21–6:9

SOME THINGS TO CONSIDER:
If you were to ask someone on the street what the Bible has to say about parent/child relationships, few would suggest it teaches, 'Dishonour and disobey your parents!' So it's probably not unexpected that Paul teaches children to obey their parents (6:1). If yesterday's verses were controversial but not yet relevant, I suspect today's verses are the opposite: not controversial, but very relevant.

Despite their relevancy, you might feel some tension with this passage. What if your parents don't seem to be worth obeying? Notice that the reason for obeying parents is not because they are inherently better than kids or deserving of obedience. We obey our parents 'in the Lord, for this is right' (6:1). Obedience flows from our commitment to Jesus. Even when your parents are being annoying or ask you to do stuff that seems pointless, you can choose to obey because you're committed to Jesus rather than committed to only doing the stuff that makes sense to you.[37]

Paul also writes that we are to honour our parents (6:2). This command is so important that God put it in the Ten Commandments with the promise of a long life if you keep it. Which doesn't mean that honouring your parents guarantees you'll live to 120, but we can take from this promise that treating your parents with respect and kindness will work out well for us in the long run. So it's worth reflecting on how we can honour our parents, not just with obedience but with the words we say to them and about them, and the way we respond to them, even when they exasperate us.

Speaking of exasperation, the wonderful thing about this passage is that the commands go both ways. Paul tells fathers to not exasperate their children, which means to make them annoyed or angry (6:4). (While he writes to fathers, these days we could apply what he says to both parents.) When Ephesians was written, fathers carried a huge amount of authority in their families. Children were expected to obey their father

---

37. Of course, obedience doesn't mean doing things which will hurt you, or putting up with abuse. If you think your parents might be treating you in ways that aren't right, you should talk to a few adults who you trust. They can help you figure out how to get help.

Day Thirty-five: Parents Can Be Exasperating

their entire life. In Roman society, a father had total authority over his children, even to the point of legally being allowed to execute them if they displeased him. So Paul continues to upend the power structures of his day with his revolutionary instructions. He says that fathers are not to wield their absolute authority with impunity, but must be respectful of the needs and feelings of their children. They are to love their children by raising them to know the good news of Jesus. Powerful men are to submit themselves to the needs of children.

While, thankfully, parents may not put their children to death anymore, Paul's instructions still carry weight. How many parents exasperate their kids for no good reason? I reckon you could think of a few times you've been exasperated in the past week! Parents live out their Spirit-filled commitment to Jesus by being kind to their kids and raising them to know Jesus.

I currently have a nine-month-old baby, so I've been thinking a lot about how to bring her up in the training and instruction of the Lord (6:4).[38] This doesn't feel too hard while she's so young. At the moment, my wife and I are establishing a habit by reading a kids' Bible and praying with her every night. But as she gets older, we'll need to be thoughtful and intentional about teaching her about Jesus, praying with her, and helping her see how the gospel affects every part of her life. I

---

38. If you remember back to Day Three, I mentioned that my wife was pregnant with our first child. The fact that baby Layla is now nine months old might give you some indication about how slowly I have been writing this book. It turns out having a baby is not conducive to book writing. By the time I get this published she'll probably be living on Mars with her grandchildren or something.

really hope we can do a good job of this for her, and I hope your parents do that for you.

However, I know some parents aren't excellent at teaching their kids about Jesus, even if they are Christians. This could be because they don't know how or find it awkward to bring up issues of faith. If that's your experience, one way you can honour them is by asking them to help you grow in your faith. You can ask them questions about what they believe or how they have seen God at work in their life. When you have a problem, ask for their wisdom and if they can pray with you. Sometimes parents feel unsure about what to do with their teenagers. If you ask for their guidance, hopefully your parents will be delighted, and will be eager to help you grow in your faith.

If your parents aren't Christians, they probably haven't raised you to know Jesus, but you can still honour them by obeying them, praying for them, and being kind even when they're being exasperating. The way you love them will show them a little of what it means to follow Jesus. What an opportunity you have to show them the love of Jesus!

As you can see, this passage may not be controversial, but it still packs a punch. If kids and parents live out their faith by loving each other, it will transform their relationships and be a witness to Jesus' love. The relationship revolution continues.

Day Thirty-five: Parents Can Be Exasperating

SOMETHING TO REFLECT ON:
When do you find it hardest to honour and obey your parents? How is God calling you to respond in love and submission out of reverence to Christ?

SOMETHING TO DO:
Do one thing today to honour your parents, whether that's obeying them in a way you have been resisting, asking for their spiritual guidance, or something else entirely. Remember that you can choose to do this out of your love for Jesus.

A PRAYER TO PRAY:
Our Father in heaven, thank you that you love us as our perfect Father. Thank you that Jesus the Son shows us how to be your child and a child of earthly parents. Please give me what I need to follow in his footsteps.

DAY THIRTY-SIX

Slavery

FOCUS VERSES: EPHESIANS 6:5–9

READ: Ephesians 5:21–6:9

SOME THINGS TO CONSIDER:
Oh no! It turns out yesterday was only a brief rest from the controversy. Today's difficult Bible topic is slavery. Hurrah!

So, I guess the question is, how should we respond when we read a passage about slavery in the Bible? Should we reject the entire Bible, because if it condones slavery, it is obviously a dangerous piece of ancient literature, intent on oppressing the weak and propping up the powerful?

Alternatively, perhaps we could reject just part of the Bible, because clearly God wouldn't condone slavery, so this passage mustn't be God's word. And while we're doing that, maybe we could find a few more passages that seem somewhat iffy that we could take out of the Bible too.

Or, perhaps there is more going on here than there seems to be at first glance. One of the important things to keep in mind is context. The world that Paul was writing in was full of slavery. Slavery in those days was not racial, like it was when people were being kidnapped from Africa and forced to work for wealthy white people. In the world of the Ephesians, anyone could become a slave. This might be through selling yourself to pay off a debt, being captured by a conquering army, or being born as the child of a slave. Slaves were not just used for menial labour, they could be doctors, teachers, or even youth pastors. (Okay, maybe not youth pastors.) Now this is not to say that slavery was okay, only that it was different from how we often think about it today. Slaves were often regarded as not fully human, and could be terribly punished, sexually assaulted, and otherwise abused. It is always a terrible thing for one person to own another.

If all this is true, you may wonder why Paul didn't just come right out and condemn slavery? One Bible scholar has likened slavery in the ancient world to electricity in today's world. People were so reliant on slavery that a leader in a small, upstart religion attempting to abolish slavery would be as effective as the pastor of a megachurch today standing up and telling the world to stop using anything electronic – it would be absurd and totally unsuccessful. There are billions of people around the world who believe we should stop using fossil fuels,

Day Thirty-six: Slavery

and yet we still don't seem to have the political will to get it done. So there is little chance Paul would have been able to abolish slavery even if he'd wanted to. But what is revolutionary about Ephesians, and the early church in general, is that slaves and masters were treated as equals. As we read in this passage, they both have responsibilities to the other. The slave was to respect their master, but the master was to do the same to the slave (6:9a)! There was no distinction in value or humanity, both were equal before God (6:9b). That Paul is even addressing slaves shows they were regarded both as full members of the church and humans created in the image of God. These were revolutionary ideas that sowed the seeds for the eventual outlawing of slavery throughout the world, even if it took way too long to happen.

So should we delete this passage from the Bible? No. Now that we know the context, we can see how God was at work in it, demonstrating how the good news of Jesus transforms even the most destructive of human relationships. Plus, as we look across history, we can see how God uses passages like this one to transform the world and empower those people who continue to fight against slavery today.

All that said, what does this passage mean for us? I'm hoping none of you are slaves.[39] But that doesn't mean there aren't people in charge of you. You probably go to school and you may have a job. In those places, people will have authority over you. How should you respond?

---

39. That said, there are still tens of millions of people in the world today who are held in slavery or forced labour. This is a terrible injustice which we cannot ignore.

You could rebel against them, especially if you have a terrible teacher or awful boss. There are plenty of both around. Or you could obey them, doing what they ask, even when they're not watching, because you know that ultimately you serve Jesus and not them (9:6–8). Wouldn't it be great if Christians were known as the best workers, because we do our best for Jesus?

What this passage also means is, even if you're not anyone's boss, you can treat everyone with kindness and respect. If the people who have the lowest status in earthly terms matter to God, then we have no reason to mistreat them. The people who serve you – cleaners, bus drivers, delivery workers – are precious and loved by God, and we have an obligation to treat them the way we would like to be treated.

Ultimately, we see in Jesus' life someone with total power who became a servant on our behalf, even to the point of dying for us. The service of Jesus dignifies our service, and all those who serve us. We serve others and love those who serve us, because we have a Saviour who serves and loves us.

SOMETHING TO REFLECT ON:
If Jesus were your teacher or boss, how would that change the way you approached your work?

SOMETHING TO DO:
Take some time today to pay attention to the people who serve you. Make eye contact and thank them. Remember, they are as precious to God as you are.

Day Thirty-six: Slavery

A PRAYER TO PRAY:

Almighty God, thank you that Jesus chose to serve us. Help me serve him as my true master, as I seek to love and serve others.

DAY THIRTY-SEVEN

Stand Your Ground

FOCUS VERSES: EPHESIANS 6:10–13

READ: Ephesians 6:10–24

SOME THINGS TO CONSIDER:
In many good action movies, the climax of the film is an enormous battle between the goodies and the baddies. At the end of the battle, the hero comes up against the biggest baddie who they thoroughly defeat, unless the creators want to leave room for a sequel, in which case the death of the villain is somewhat ambiguous.

I always find these scenes exciting! Especially when the battle looks like all is lost, and an unexpected ally turns up to lend a hand, and suddenly the hero has exactly what they need to win.

Despite how exciting I find action movies, I don't know how excited I'd be if I were in a battle in real life. However, as we get to the final verses of Ephesians, that's exactly where we find ourselves – in a battle. Or rather, we discover that we have always been in a battle, whether or not we like it. This is the ultimate battle of good and evil in the heavenly realms, and here on earth. It is the battle between God, his spiritual forces, and people, against Satan and all his demons.

Despite how it may sometimes feel, our enemies are not other people. They aren't the people who bully you, or say terrible things about you online. They aren't the people who believe differently to you about politics, the environment, sexuality, or gender. They aren't people at all. If they have flesh and blood, they are not our enemy (6:12). This is why Jesus can tell us to love our enemies (and here he is talking about other people), because he knows that our true enemy is all the dark forces that the devil has mustered to subvert the good work of Jesus.

Many people don't want to believe in dark spiritual forces. But if we believe in good ones, why not bad ones? When we look at the world, and see the evil and suffering, we can see the hand of Satan at work as he musters his forces to tempt and cajole people to hurt others and rebel against God. So when people attack or threaten you, and when you feel like attacking or threatening them, remember that this is Satan at work, whispering lies as he attempts to cause division and destruction amongst humans who God dearly loves.

Day Thirty-seven: Stand Your Ground

Paul writes this part of Ephesians to encourage us to be prepared for the real battle against our actual enemies, so that in the end we might stand (6:13). Notice that the outcome for us is not to win. It is not for us to defeat Satan. Satan's defeat has already happened. Jesus defeated him at the cross when he died for us, taking the curse of sin upon himself and rising again, winning us new life. At that moment, Jesus defeated and humiliated Satan and his forces (Colossians 2:13–15).

So while we're on the winning side, our job is not to win, but only to stand. To stand means that at the end of the battle we have remained faithful to Jesus. This might seem simple enough, but you only have to look at how many people start the journey of following Jesus, only to leave along the way. If you want to stand for Jesus till the very end, then you better pay attention to what follows.

The matters that Paul has discussed in Ephesians – how we live faithfully in our words and actions; how we live out our sexuality, and deal with our anger; how we treat others and engage in our relationships – these are not just matters of individual morality, but part of our fight against the powers of evil. Remaining faithful in these things is what it means to stand. Faithfulness to Jesus is not just an abstract concept, or a feeling in your heart, it is the day in, day out commitment to live in a way the honours Jesus – loving God and loving others.

If this seems a little overwhelming, do not be concerned. We aren't sent into this battle unprepared, like soldiers in our underwear. We are given the armour we need for the fight. What is this armour? That is what we will look at tomorrow.

For now, remember, you have been called to stand your ground, and you can. You are on the winning side, with the victory already assured, standing in God's mighty power. You have a Father who loves you, a Saviour who has given his life for you, a Spirit who lives in you, and the amour of God to equip you. 'When the day of evil comes, you [will] be able to stand your ground, and after you have done everything, to stand' (6:13).

SOMETHING TO REFLECT ON:
As you look at your life, where do you notice Satan and his forces attacking and tempting you the most? What might it look like to resist him and stand for Jesus?

SOMETHING TO DO:
Share with a Christian friend where you are being tempted by Satan the most. Ask them to pray with you for strength. Ask how you can pray for them.

A PRAYER TO PRAY:
Victorious God, thank you that you have already won the war against the powers of evil in the heavenly realms. Please help me to remember Jesus' victory at the cross on our behalf and rely on your strength as I stand against the devil and the forces of evil.

DAY THIRTY-EIGHT

Armour Up!

FOCUS VERSES: EPHESIANS 6:14–17

READ: Ephesians 6:10–24

SOME THINGS TO CONSIDER:
One of the toys I most wanted as a kid was a suit of armour. Those plastic sets that were sold in toy stores, with a breastplate, helmet, shield, belt, and best of all, a sword in its scabbard. When I was at friends' places and they had one of these sets of toy armour, I would find any excuse to play with it. The helmet was always uncomfortable, the belt didn't do up properly, and the sword was flimsy and usually broken. But having that armour, I felt like a magnificent knight who could fight villains and rescue anyone in distress. As a kid who loved this kind of thing, you can probably guess

that I loved it whenever we looked at today's passage in Sunday school.

Happily for that armour-loving kid in me, I still enjoy this passage. While we don't get to wear physical armour as Christians (which is probably a good thing because we'd look weird, and Christians wielding weapons is almost always a bad thing), this armour that Paul describes is a lot more useful in our life, anyway. Paul is describing how we can use the basic tenets of the Christian life to be equipped to stand firm in God's mighty power.

So what are the parts of the armour of God?[40]

First, there is the belt of truth. Satan's greatest mode of attack is lies (see John 8:44; Revelation 12:9). It was Satan's lies which led to Adam and Eve's first sin in the garden, and he's been lying ever since. So we put on the belt by remembering and speaking the truth. We remember the truth of who God is, what Jesus has done for us, and who we are in him as God's loved, saved children. We also live lives of truth, because when we lie to ourself or others, we speak Satan's native language, and we give him a chance to wreak havoc in our lives.

Next, there is the breastplate of righteousness. A breastplate protects our vital organs. Jesus has given us his righteousness, that is, his perfect moral standing before God, through his death on the cross. Satan may accuse us of evil, but our evil has been paid for. We are protected by

---

40. If you've looked closely at the cover of this book, you may have noticed that the girl is not wearing conventional armour. She is wearing what looks like a hoodie, jeans, and Converse hi-tops. This outfit is pretty much my daily uniform, because it's so darn comfy. But please just assume that she's wearing an armoured hoodie, jeans, and hi-tops, because she wants to be both comfy *and* awesome as she stands in God's power.

Day Thirty-eight: Armour Up!

the work of Jesus. We put on the breastplate by trusting in Jesus' righteousness, not our own.

Then there are the shoes, our 'feet fitted with the readiness that comes from the gospel of peace' (6:15). We can stand firm in the face of Satan's attacks because we know the good news that God has made peace with us through Jesus. We can also always be ready to share this good news with others, so God might rescue them too from the grips of evil.

We have the shield of faith. We are protected from Satan's flaming arrows of accusation and temptation by having faith that draws on the promises and character of God to protect us in times of doubt and trouble.

We wear the helmet of salvation. Helmets are good for keeping your head safe and are pretty important for staying alive. They also allow you to keep your head up so you can see where you're going, and not have to be constantly crouching in fear. Knowing you are saved by God from sin and will be safe on the final day means you can hold your head up in the spiritual battle, confident in God's power.

Finally, we have 'the sword of the Spirit, which is the word of God' (6:17). This is the only piece of armour with which we attack. It's used for close-up combat – it's not the rocket launcher of the Spirit, because Satan's attacks are personal. How do we defend against Satan's lies? We wield the truth of God's word. When Satan tempted Jesus in the desert, Jesus quoted the Bible at him (see Matthew 4:1–11). Jesus wielded the sword of the Spirit to protect himself, and we can do the same. When we know our Bible, and the truth it contains, we can bring it to mind, even speak it out loud, when we are tempted to sin or to believe lies. We can also use it when Satan accuses us or tries to make us doubt God's love for us. With the word of God, we can defeat Satan's attacks, standing firm in God's mighty power.

So that's the armour of God. You don't need to be a special Christian to get it. Any Christian who knows the gospel has what they need. As you are established in the good news of Jesus and all that it means, you are equipped to stand firm from now until Jesus returns.

SOMETHING TO REFLECT ON:
Spend some time reflecting on the good news of what Jesus' death and resurrection means for you and all Christians. As you do this, remind yourself of how this good news equips you to stand firm against Satan and in your faithfulness to Jesus.

SOMETHING TO DO:
Choose a favourite verse from Ephesians to memorise. Spend time over the next few days memorising it so that you might be better able to use the sword of the Spirit.

A PRAYER TO PRAY:
Powerful God, thank you that you have given us everything we need to stand firm in your power. Help me put on the whole armour that you provide in your gospel, so that in knowing you better, I might stand against Satan's lies and schemes.

DAY THIRTY-NINE

Supply Lines

FOCUS VERSES: EPHESIANS 6:18–20

READ: Ephesians 6:10–24

SOME THINGS TO CONSIDER:
When we hear war stories about famous battles and feats of heroism, almost all happen at the front lines – when combatants meet each other, shots are fired, and bombs are dropped. However, what we rarely tell stories about are the logistics that are necessary to fight a war. If an army goes into battle, there are countless more people behind the front line whose jobs are to equip those who are fighting. They work to send food, ammunition, and fuel, to build the equipment, and make the uniforms. A military without supplies will not last long. This is why, in wartime, each side will often attempt to cut off the

opposing forces' supply lines. According to one logistics expert, in World War II, the allied forces sunk over four times as many Japanese supply ships as naval ships. This meant that by the end of the war, the Japanese Navy and Air Force had little of the fuel they needed to operate and could not fight against the allied forces.[41]

I'm telling you all this because in today's passage, Paul gives us the last of his instructions for life on the spiritual battlefield, and the message is: pray! Prayer is our supply line as we face Satan and his cronies. No matter how spiritually powerful we might be, Satan is much more powerful than us. But don't worry – because of Jesus, he doesn't have power over us. Through prayer, we don't stand against the powers of darkness in our own strength. Prayer is tapping in to God's mighty power. That's why we pray, so that God can supply us with what we need.

In verse 18, Paul outlines four ways we need to be praying: on all occasions, with all kinds of prayers, always praying, for all the Lord's people. That's a lot of alls! It's clear how important prayer is.

'On all occasions' because every situation could use some prayer. Are you tempted to sin? Pray for help. Is someone you know sick? Pray for healing. Has something wonderful happened? Pray and give thanks to God. Have you done something wrong? Pray for forgiveness. Do you have a big decision to make? Pray for wisdom. Pray when you're alone, pray with your friends, pray with your

---

41. Cliff Wellborn, 'Supply Line Warfare.' *Army Logistician* 40, no. 6 (December 2008). http://web.archive.org/web/20190405015441/https://almc.army.mil/alog/issues/NovDec08/spplyline_war.html.

Day Thirty-nine: Supply Lines

family, pray in a crowd, pray when things start, and pray when things end. Pray on all occasions.

'With all kinds of prayers and requests' because no one prayer fits all. We should pray to praise God for who he is and what he has done. We should pray to confess our sins. We should pray to thank God for what he has done for us. We should pray to ask God for what we need. We can even pray just to say 'hello'. Even when we feel we must pray but we don't know what to pray, just groan, yell, or make some other noise, and let the Holy Spirit translate what you need to say to God. He's good like that (see Romans 8:26).

'Always keep on praying' doesn't mean that we must only pray and do nothing else, but there is never a point when you are finished praying. Just as you may be constantly in a conversation with your friends, either over text, in person, online, or just sharing looks across a classroom, the same is true with our prayers. We're always in need of God's power, so we must always be in conversation with him.

'For all the Lord's people' because you are not in this fight alone. We follow Jesus with others, so we should make sure our prayers are not just about ourselves and our lives. Instead, we must remember to pray for our fellow Christians who stand alongside us. For the Christians we know in our church, youth group, and school. We can pray for Christians around the world who are being persecuted for their faith, those who are seeking to share the good news of Jesus, and Christians who are struggling to stay faithful to Jesus. You can even take some time to learn what life is like for Christians in different parts of the world, so you can better pray for them.

Finally, in verses 19 and 20, Paul asks for prayer that he might share the mystery of the gospel fearlessly (check out Day Sixteen if you want to refresh yourself on what Paul means by 'mystery'). Even as Paul is a prisoner because of his faith, he asks for prayers for boldness. You would think he could just have a rest, content that he's done enough. But he is committed to preaching the good news till his dying breath. Paul was a pretty bold guy. He faced the most powerful and violent people and yet still shared God's message with them. His boldness came because he prayed and because he had others praying for him. As he tells us in 2 Corinthians 12:9, God's power is made perfect in weakness. Paul may be weak, but because he knows his weakness he relies on Jesus, which makes him strong.

We too must seek prayer from others as we follow Jesus. We need his strength to be faithful to him, to stand against Satan's schemes, and to share boldly the good news of what Jesus has done. When we pray, God will supply what we need.

SOMETHING TO REFLECT ON:
When in your life do you need boldness to share God's goodness faithfully?

SOMETHING TO DO:
For the next week, set multiple alarms each day to remind you to pray. Each time your alarm goes off, pray about

Day Thirty-nine: Supply Lines

whatever situation you are in, in whatever way seems appropriate.

A PRAYER TO PRAY:
Giving God, thank you that you supply all my needs. Help me pray so that I am relying on you and not myself.

DAY FORTY

The End Credits

FOCUS VERSES: EPHESIANS 6:21–24

READ: Ephesians 6:10–24

SOME THINGS TO CONSIDER:
If you're like me, you may be tempted to skip these last few verses as unimportant, like I select 'play next episode' to skip the end credits of TV shows. But if 'all Scripture is God-breathed' (2 Timothy 3:16) then even these verses are from God.

We have discussed context a bit in these devotions, and verse 21 is a clear example of why you cannot take whatever is written in the Bible and apply it directly to your life. Because if you were to do that, you would expect Tychicus to personally tell you everything that Paul is up to these days. If Tychicus was secretly Nicolas Flamel and discovered the secret of immortality, I assume his update would be pretty dull: 'Yep. Still dead.'

So what do we see in this passage? First, that Paul didn't do his ministry alone. Because he was stuck in prison, he had faithful Christians serving him, and in turn, serving the church. If you were a prisoner in Rome, you weren't fed, clothed, or cared for by your guards. You needed your friends and family to look after you. Tychicus, as well as a bunch of others mentioned in the New Testament, served Paul by visiting him, bringing him what he needed, and delivering his letters. Ephesians is a wonderful book, but it would have been useless if it had just stayed with Paul. Tychicus would have delivered this letter to the Ephesian churches, as well as Colossians to the church in Colossae (see Colossians 4:7–9). He also would have been called upon to answer questions from the church members about Paul and the content of the letter. We're able to read Ephesians today because of Tychicus' commitment to serving Paul and his ministry.

Serving Jesus and his people is not meant to be an extraordinary life full of heroic feats, courageous preaching, and extreme persecution. For some, it may be that, but for many, serving Jesus is full of smaller, everyday acts of love: visiting someone in need, preparing a meal for someone, delivering a message, cleaning up a mess, being a caring friend to the lonely. The kingdom of God runs on small but magnificent acts of love. We cannot all lead lives like Paul (in fact, there was only one Paul), but we can choose to be like Tychicus, seeing a need and meeting it in whatever way we are able.

Day Forty: The End Credits

Finally, Paul closes the letter with a blessing of three big themes from Ephesians: peace, love, and grace (6:23–24). Peace, because, as we have read, we have a Saviour in Jesus who has made peace between us and God, and who makes peace between us and our enemies too, by bringing us all into God's heavenly family. Love, because it is God's love that has saved us, and it is God's love which enables us to love others and keeps his people unified. And grace, because it is by grace we have been saved. Everything we receive from God is an unearned gift. May we rely on God's grace, rather than our efforts.

And so we've made it to the end of Ephesians! As you've read the book, I hope you've been moved by the love of God, the grace of our Lord Jesus, and the power of the Holy Spirit, so that you might better live a life of faithfulness and commitment to God and his people.

'Peace to the brothers and sisters, and love with faith from God the Father and the Lord Jesus Christ. Grace to all who love our Lord Jesus Christ with an undying love' (6:23–24).

SOMETHING TO REFLECT ON:
If we don't have to lead an extraordinary life, but can serve Jesus with everyday acts of love, what would your ordinary, but magnificent, life look like?

SOMETHING TO DO:
Think back to the most important things God has taught you through reading Ephesians. You may like to write these things down. If, on Day One, you wrote what you

were hoping God might say to you, compare what you wrote then with what you have heard from God now that you have finished working through Ephesians.

A PRAYER TO PRAY:

God of peace, love, and grace, thank you that in Jesus you have made peace with us, you have shown us your love, and you have given us your grace. Help me know your peace, love, and grace to live a life of love in your kingdom.

Bibliography

If I wrote anything particularly impressive in these books it was definitely because of the Holy Spirit, and probably also because I had a lot of help from people smarter and wiser than me. I've done a lot of teaching on Ephesians over the years, and heard even more sermons and talks, so I don't remember where I learnt everything I know about the book. However, what follows are some of the main resources I used while preparing these devotions. If you were to read any one of these books, I'm sure it'd be very useful in helping you understand, enjoy, and be challenged by Ephesians.

Bruce, F. F. *The Epistle to the Ephesians: A Verse-by-Verse Exposition*. London: Pickering & Inglis, 1977.

Calvin, John. *Commentary on Ephesians*, n.d.

Coekin, Richard. *Ephesians for You*. Epsom: The Good Book Company, 2015.

Cohick, Lynn H. *Ephesians: A New Covenant Commentary*. New Covenant Commentary Series. Eugene: Cascade Books, 2010.

Dunnam, Maxie D. *Galatians, Ephesians, Philippians, Colossians, Philemon*. Nashville: Thomas Nelson, 1982.

Hawthorne, Gerald F., Ralph P. Martin, and Daniel G. Reid, eds. *Dictionary of Paul and His Letters*. Downers Grove: InterVarsity Press, 1993.

O'Brien, Peter T. *The Letter to the Ephesians*. The Pillar New Testament Commentary. Grand Rapids: Eerdmans, 2009.[42]

Rasmussen, Carl. *Zondervan Atlas of the Bible*. Rev. ed. Grand Rapids: Zondervan, 2010.

Snodgrass, Klyne. *Ephesians. The NIV Application Commentary*. Grand Rapids: Zondervan, 1996.

Stott, John R. W. *The Message of Ephesians: God's New Society*. The Bible Speaks Today. Leicester: InterVarsity Press, 1991.

Wright, Tom. *Paul for Everyone: The Prison Letters: Ephesians, Philippians, Colossians, and Philemon*. London: SPCK, 2004.

---

42. This commentary by O'Brien has been acknowledged to contain plagiarism. It's a good book with some bad referencing. So I'm also indebted to the people who were not properly referenced in the writing of this commentary.

Get more Pop's Devotions

Do you ever feel less than heroic in your faith?

Jonah is the prophet for you. He's a scared, overly-emotional, responsibility-avoiding, anti-hero of biblical proportions. As you struggle with how to respond to your calling, how to treat your enemies, your disappointment with God, and how to escape the belly of a giant fish, these devotions with Jonah will challenge, encourage, and delight you.

Pop's Devotions is a series of engaging daily devotions, written for young people, that works through books of the Bible from beginning to end.

Buy now at tomfrench.com.au

Also by Tom French

'Grab this book with both hands and see where it takes you!'
Ali Martin, Soul Survivor UK

Ultimate fighting bears, a fat king who poops himself, zombies, donkey 'bits', and a fart.

These are not the things you'd expect to find in the Bible, but they're all there. If you thought the Bible was dull, think again. This is your chance to discover all the parts of the Bible they don't teach you in Sunday school – but probably should.

Weird, Crude, Funny, and Nude is a hilarious, Christ-centred, and somewhat inappropriate look at some of the least known and discussed parts of the Bible – perfect for teenagers or any of us who think nudity, poop, and farts are funny.

Buy now at tomfrench.com.au

'*A Dozen Disappointing Disciples* is funny, easy to read, relevant, accessible, and thought-provoking.'

Chris Morphew, author of *Best News Ever* and the Big Questions series

**Matthew was a traitor.
James and John wanted to blow up innocent people.
Thomas doubted Jesus rose from the dead.
Peter chopped off a guy's ear, then denied he even knew Jesus.**

Jesus' disciples were intolerant, selfish, violent, and dull. They were exactly the sorts of people you would think God couldn't use. Except that he did, and they changed the world. *A Dozen Disappointing Disciples* is an engaging, and often hilarious, look at the stupid stuff the twelve disciples did. You'll discover how Jesus used them, and how he can use you too. Fun, encouraging, and challenging, this book will help you see that not even your stupidity is any match for the power of Jesus.

Buy now at tomfrench.com.au

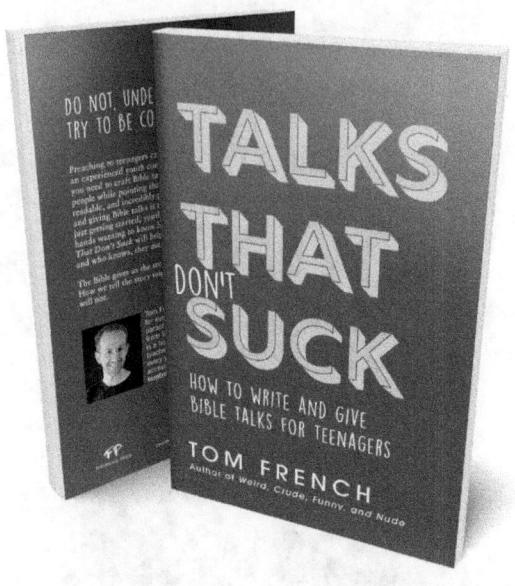

'Do not, under any circumstances, try to be cooler than you are.'

Preaching to teenagers can be a terrifying prospect. Tom French, an experienced youth communicator, will give you everything you need to craft Bible talks that engage and challenge young people while pointing them to the love of God in Jesus. This fun, readable, and incredibly practical step-by-step guide for writing and giving Bible talks is the ideal book for new youth leaders just getting started, youth pastors looking for a refresher, or old hands wanting to know how to speak to young people. *Talks That Don't Suck* will help you ensure your talks aren't terrible – and who knows, they may even be amazing!

The Bible gives us the story for all people, for all generations. How we tell the story might change, but the truth of the story will not.

Buy now at tomfrench.com.au

About the Author

Tom French is married to his excellent wife, Emily Sandrussi. He is also a youth ministry veteran, having spent the past two decades working with teenagers in churches and schools around Australia. Every year he teaches the Bible to thousands of young people in youth groups, churches, schools, and camps around the country. He has a Bachelor of Theology from Sydney Missionary and Bible College.

Tom lives in Melbourne with Emily and their daughter, Layla. You can often find him on his couch eating popcorn for dinner.

Visit **tomfrench.com.au** to receive a free ebook, blog updates, and the latest on new books. There you can also listen to Tom's sermons, book Tom to speak, see a photo of Tom holding a microphone, and much more.

YouTube: **youtube.com/twfrench**
Instagram: **@twfrench**
Facebook: **facebook.com/twfrench**

Podcast: Search for **'Tom French Preaching'** in your favourite podcast app

www.ingramcontent.com/pod-product-compliance
Lightning Source LLC
Chambersburg PA
CBHW070252010526
44107CB00056B/2438